Age Gets Better with Wine

D1007698

Age Gets Better with Wine

New Science for a Healthier,
Better, and Longer Life

Richard A. Baxter, M.D.

Copyright © 2009 by Richard A. Baxter, M.D..

Library of Congress Control Number: 20Q9928716
ISBN: 978-1-934259-24-5

All rights reserved. No part of this book may be reproduced or transmitted in
any form or by any means, electronic or mechanical, including photocopying,
recording, or by any information storage and retrieval system, without
permission in writing from the copyright owner.

This book is about healthy living, but it is not intended to diagnose, treat, or
prevent disease and is not a substitute for consultation with a physician. While
I have tried to provide sound advice, and interpret the studies upon which this
book is based with accuracy, what you do with it is entirely up to you.

This book was printed in the United States of America.

To order additional copies of this book, contact:
The Wine Appreciation Guild
360 Swift Avenue
South San Francisco, CA 94080
(650) 866-3020
www.wineappreciation.com

Contents

Disclaimer

This book is about healthy living, but it is not intended to diagnose, treat, or prevent disease and is not a substitute for consultation with a physician. While I have tried to provide sound advice, and interpret the studies upon which this book is based with accuracy, what you do with it is entirely up to you.

Acknowledgements

The nature of this subject requires that I borrow from the many researchers and others whose work forms the foundation of this book. There are thousands of published papers on the subject of wine and health, hence it is impossible to adequately recognize all who have contributed to the field, and inaccuracies are inevitable. Certain controversies are also unavoidable, and no doubt some will take issue with my interpretations, and perhaps question my forays into their areas of expertise. I don't claim to speak authoritatively about cardiology, or cancer, or neurology, or any of the other biomedical specialties outside of my own as a plastic surgeon, but there are precious few who do come forth to engage in serious discussion of the wine issue from an anti-aging perspective. My hope here is to stimulate such a dialogue.

We do not lack for giants, however, on whose shoulders the world of wine and health research has been hoisted. These include R. Curtis Ellison of Boston, Arthur Klatsky of Kaiser-Permanente in California, Serge Renaud of Bordeaux, and Morten Grønbaeck of Denmark. Their lesser-known predecessors deserve their due as well; among these are Salvatore Lucia, a University of California Medical Center (San Francisco) professor who authored the book *Wine as Food and Medicine* in 1954, and the late Gene Ford who wrote *The Science of Healthy Drinking* and whose work was prodigious and seminal. Others are increasingly taking up the call and we are all in their debt.

A toast: Preface to the second edition

A lot has happened since the first edition. The wine-health connection story has gone mainstream, with almost daily press releases about the newest study on wine and Alzheimer's or cancer, or the newest pill containing wine-derived substances claiming miraculous benefits. At least one large biotech company, Sirtris, was founded based on the promise of developing anti-aging and anti-disease pharmaceuticals from wine-derived substances, and their progress has been so remarkable that they were acquired by GlaxoSmithKline in early 2008 for more than $700 million. Resveratrol, the most widely known (if also among the most difficult to pronounce) wine compound, is available in supplement pills in grocery stores and from dozens of internet-based vendors. It appears in everything from skin care products to sports drinks. In a few short years it has nearly become a household word, yet it remains just as widely misunderstood, so I have added an entire chapter on resveratrol.

Clearly, something big is happening here. I see it as nothing less than the beginning of a whole new conception of nutritional science, a rethinking of our approach to food, drink, health, and aging. The fascinating properties of these wine compounds are defining a new field of biology, bringing legitimacy to the science of anti-aging. With every step forward, though, we look back and see the insights that our ancestors had about wine and health for millennia. We are rediscovering our past even as we open the door to the future. We find that traditional ways offer wisdom and guidance to a scientific quest immensely more sophisticated than could be imagined only a couple of generations past.

What emerges from the clamor of so much attention, so much noise in the media and the marketplace, is not only the picture of wine as a healthy thing, but also the innate human tendency to oversimplify the situation: just put it in a pill, I'm too busy to have wine with dinner. Try Googling "resveratrol" and you will find dozens, if not hundreds, of purveyors touting the particular benefits of their supplement formula. But here's the rub: although there are thousands of research papers from prestigious institutions around the world contributing to the wine-health story, there are virtually none confirming that these compounds do the same thing in pill form in humans. That may very well eventually turn out to be the case, or at least we may find that there are some measurable benefits, but despite all this momentum we just aren't there yet. The benefits of wine aren't attributable to a single molecule out of the thousands, and out of the context of a meal. An analogous account is the surprising finding that taking vitamin supplements may actually do more harm than good, a consensus view among experts now. It just isn't the same as eating whole foods and drinking real wine. Some may see irony in the finding that it is the modern science of molecular biology in all its exquisite detail that brings us back to customs dating to primitive times, but I view it as immensely reassuring.

This edition is extensively updated with new findings based on the latest research. The references section has been expanded and should be a useful tool for clinicians and anyone interested in more detail. Admittedly, the pace of research is such now that a claim of being fully up to date is not realistic, but in general it is fair to assert that the picture painted in the first edition is reinforced and clarified. The premise that wine, red wine in particular, holds the key to understanding and intervening in age-related disease and decline is assembled around an increasingly solid framework. But the more I read the current biomedical literature, the more I gain respect for all those who have contributed to the topic of wine and healthy living for a great many years, and so I have added more historical vignettes as well. This new scientific construct, wine as a biochemical fountain of youth, is built over a deep well and upon a broad foundation. Wine is our touchstone for a traditional way of living in a modern world.

I do recommend that you enjoy a glass or two of red wine as you read this. After all, the case will be made herein that wine makes you smart, through specific chemical reactions in the brain. And keeping the brain engaged is one of the most effective anti-aging exercises you can do. So here is the perfect opportunity to rediscover what you really knew all along: that living well, enjoying life, and living smart are all mutually reinforcing. To your health!

Wine was created from the beginning to make men joyful.
—Ecclesiasticus XXXI-35

Aperitif

Jeanne Calment passed quietly in her sleep in Arles, France in early August 1997, after a life spanning nearly 123 years. She had long become one of the world's most reluctant celebrities, simply for having lived longer than any other human in recorded history. She was born in the nineteenth century in the same year as the composer Maurice Ravel, and witnessed the completion of the Eiffel Tower. Her birth predated the invention of the telephone, and her death was announced globally via the internet. As a young woman she sold art supplies to Van Gogh and other "radical" impressionist artists making the pilgrimage to the light of Provence. She embraced the simple art of living, and the long trajectory of her life inspired generations of scientists seeking to unlock the mysteries of extreme longevity.

At age 90, she had made a deal with her lawyer who was to subsidize her apartment until she died (a "life estate"), with possession then passing to him. It might have been a profitable investment had she not outlived him, despite being decades older! He was never able to take the apartment, and in fact his heirs had to assume payments for several more years. Even a bicycle accident resulting in a leg fracture at age 100 barely slowed her down. At the age of 110 she reluctantly entered a retirement facility, the Maison du Lac, where she continued to hold forth with gusto.

Super-centenarians—that is, those who live more than 110 years—are still relatively rare, though their numbers are increasing rapidly. Jeanne Calment was one of the first to be studied, and many aspects of her life reveal common denominators that aging researchers have identified. One of these factors is the maintenance of an active mind, one which is intellectually engaged and also employs a simple *joie de vivre.* Mme. Calment certainly embodied that. Stories abound about her playfulness with the reporters who flocked to her birthday celebrations during the latter years of her life. When one of them commented "Maybe I'll see you next year" she replied "I don't see why not; you seem to be in pretty good health!"

But there is obviously more to living long and well than choosing to have a good attitude, and Mme. Calment's lifestyle choices have also been analyzed intently. Her dietary patterns were typical of what came to be called the "Mediterranean diet." Olive oil was not only a prominent dietary component but her preferred skin moisturizer as well. She had a fondness for chocolate, and didn't avoid rich foods. But her primary "weakness" was red wine, which she consumed on a daily basis for most of her life.

Within a few years of Mme. Calment's death, reports began to appear in the medical literature about a unique substance found in red wine called *resveratrol,* capable of significantly extending the lifespan of experimental organisms. When the longevity effect was demonstrated to occur in mice fed supplemental resveratrol in November of 2006, it was said to be the most widely circulated news of the day.[*] Scientists began to seriously ask whether a lifespan of 123 years might become *average.* Was red wine—with its resveratrol—along with chocolate, and the Mediterranean diet the secret to Jeanne Calment's incredible longevity?

The modern science of anti-aging has recently converged on what Jeanne Calment took as a matter of course, namely the role of red wine. Thousands of scientific studies in major peer-reviewed biomedical journals now attest to the incredible properties of red wine and its polyphenols (the anti-oxidants that are also found in chocolate and olive oil) in not only slowing aging on a fundamental level, but reducing the risk of degenerative diseases associated with aging.

This latter point is important because no one would want to live to 120 or beyond if they had to suffer with chronic health problems or Alzheimer's disease, requiring constant nursing care and disengaged from

---

[*] According to AIM Digest (AIM stands for Alcohol In Moderation), an online resource for healthy drinking science news.

the world. But this is where the wine story gets even more interesting: There is an emerging consensus that the risk of Alzheimer's disease may be reduced substantially, perhaps by up to 80%, simply by regular consumption of a glass or two of red wine with dinner. Mental function is actually enhanced and preserved with age in those who drink red wine regularly, in contradistinction to what is generally assumed and widely advised.

The salutary effects of red wine in reducing heart disease have been well publicized (the "French paradox"), but newer studies also confirming lower risk of many types of cancer defy conventional wisdom. It doesn't stop there: diabetes, obesity, pulmonary conditions, osteoporosis, kidney problems, and an ever-increasing list of disease conditions all seem to be thwarted by red wine. Even cataracts, gastric ulcers, and dental cavities are deterred by wine polyphenols. And these aren't merely statistical associations; researchers are beginning to map out in detail exactly how all of this occurs on a fundamental biologic basis.

This book is about the science of anti-aging, and the remarkable recent discoveries about resveratrol and its wine polyphenol kin. These compounds are so remarkable that when I first conceived the idea for this book I planned to call it *Vitamin W*. But vitamins each prevent a specific disease, while wine polyphenols reduce risk, sometimes dramatically, for a wide variety of degenerative conditions. Indeed, a case could be made that in a normal diet—one that is not particularly deficient in daily vitamin requirements— vitamin W polyphenols are more important than "true" vitamins in many ways. Wine isn't a nutritional supplement; it is, as we shall see, nutrition for the body and the mind.

One reason for wine's special abilities is that its polyphenol anti-oxidant properties are far greater than the anti-oxidant vitamins that are popularly used for that purpose. Since oxidative damage is believed to play a central role in aging and related diseases, the fact that wine is so potent in this regard merits a serious look. In excess, of course, wine does more harm than good, but the same is true for vitamins. (I vividly remember a patient from my medical school days who had written a book touting mega-vitamin therapy; not only did he have to undergo surgery for kidney stones caused by vitamin overuse, but his young daughter had to be hospitalized for brain swelling caused by vitamin A toxicity.) Yet the massive growth of the vitamin industry serves as a constant reminder of how we trivialize the risks and inflate the benefits of vitamin supplementation and "natural" cures.

This points to a popular tendency to oversimplify nutritional and medical science in general, fallout perhaps of our desire for an antidote to stress in the modern world. It also serves to emphasize a risk of publishing a book like this; some will apply the "if a little bit is good, then more is better" philosophy or misinterpret my intentions as blanket encouragement of alcohol abuse. Nothing could be farther from the truth. But I also believe that the medical establishment tends toward a paternalistic and overly protective attitude when it comes to the question of drinking; it has long been politically incorrect to discuss any level of consumption as possibly healthy, despite substantial and growing evidence to the contrary. For example, *not drinking* is the number two risk factor for cardiovascular disease (after smoking), but you probably haven't heard that from your health care provider. The problem isn't a lack of available data, it is getting reliable information out so people can make intelligent choices and doctors can give good advice.

Helping patients make informed decisions is central to any physician's practice ethic, regardless of specialty. As a plastic surgeon, my motivation isn't simply to do procedures that make people look better or younger, but also to learn what I can about combating the aging process itself. (There is also the element of enlightened self-interest.) In light of recent discoveries, any comprehensive study on aging is incomplete without a thorough examination of wine polyphenols. It isn't simply a question of fending off and outlasting the diseases of aging: In this book we will explore how wine polyphenols are revealing the answers to *why* and *how* we age.

This is how a plastic surgeon came to write a book about wine; anti-aging is the unifying theme across dozens of specialties that each contribute to our understanding of wine biochemistry, and vice-versa. It may seem more appropriate for a wine researcher, someone more directly involved in laboratory or clinical research in the component fields of wine and health, to have taken the lead on this subject but there are reasons why an "outsider" might be better able to bring a fresh perspective. One reason is academic independence: Researchers who are dependent upon grants to support their work generally need to avoid commercial forums and the appearance of profit or bias.

On the other hand, I have no such constraints or connections to the wine business (other than as a consumer.) Only by viewing the topic from many different angles do we see the whole picture. All of the various fields contributing to the study of wine and health—cardiology, neurology, oncology, epidemiology, biochemistry, nutritional science, and on and on—intersect at the topic of anti-aging.

The convergence of so many diverse fields has generated considerable excitement, and the pace of research is increasing dramatically. Using an online database called PubMed, which lists articles published in the biomedical sciences, it can be seen that the number of articles increased from essentially none in the early 1990's to dozens each year now; searching specifically for resveratrol, the annual numbers are in the hundreds.

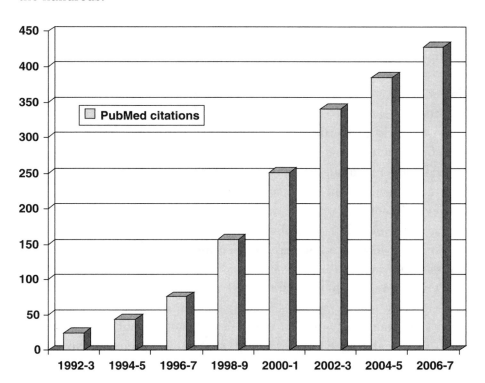

This fervor is a mixed blessing though. While it underscores the timeliness and importance of the subject of wine and health, it also means that important discoveries will have been made between the final edit and the publication of this book. The whole topic has ballooned to the point that just keeping up to date with the highlights is a challenge. But the notion that wine is good for you didn't just occur to someone in a lab last week; with some perspective, it becomes more of a question of why it took us so long to appreciate it. Here we will provide the foundation of knowledge and the tools needed in order to gain that perspective.

As a surgeon, I am also uniquely positioned to see the downside of alcohol consumption, and my intent here is to be balanced. Over the course of my surgical career and training, I have performed reconstructive surgery on children with birth defects from fetal alcohol syndrome, treated facial trauma from domestic violence and drunken driving, and cared for patients hemorrhaging from alcoholic liver disease. The social effects of excessive drinking are enormous, and none of this should be taken lightly. Yet it is increasingly apparent that, on a net public health basis, the positive effects of red wine in moderation are vastly greater. It is important at the outset to distinguish between regular consumption of wine with meals, and the destructive behaviors associated with alcohol abuse. They are not the same and do not overlap.

Such is the central conundrum with this topic: polyphenols, with their manifold properties, aren't the whole story. Alcohol has its own benefits, which are measurable and real. It is the interaction between the two components, along with concomitant dietary and lifestyle elements that creates the alchemy of a healthy and long life. The health and longevity benefits of wine cannot be extracted entirely out of their place in a healthy lifestyle and applied in isolation. Moderation, and a context of wine as a food, are inseparable from the longevity effect. There are, however, alternative dietary sources of "wine" polyphenols, so those who don't drink or shouldn't on a frequent basis can still apply the wisdom of wine to good benefit.

Even though research on the area of wine polyphenols is ongoing and even escalating, each new report must be interpreted in the context of previously published work. The scientific method requires objectivity and independence, and it is easy to be led astray in a complex topic such as the epidemiology and biochemistry of anti-aging and wine. At times it seems like a minefield of competing commercial interests, biases, moral pronouncements, and a multitude of misconceptions. So think of this book as your map through the terrain and a safety manual for healthy living and maximum enjoyment of life. It's an age-old formula for a rich old age, one thousands of years in the making.

Good wine is a necessity of life for me.

—Thomas Jefferson

Chapter 1

History and Hysteria:
Wine and Health Through the Ages

Wine, the most delightful of drinks, whether we owe it to Noah, who planted the vine, or to Bacchus, who pressed juice from the grape, goes back to the childhood of the world.

—Brillat-Savarin

Winemaking is older than recorded history, and the story of wine is embedded in the foundations of civilization. Wine has been associated with health and anti-aging properties from Neolithic times to the present day, though only recently have these beliefs been buttressed with scientific scrutiny. Considering how difficult the exigencies of daily life were in those primitive times, the discovery of wine must have seemed truly mystical. No doubt those entrusted with the special knowledge required in order to make and store wine held elevated status in early communities, and it is perhaps only a modest exaggeration to say that the first shamans were just possibly Cro-Magnon *vignerons*.

Because wine does have certain healing properties, and the ability to sooth the injured and alleviate distress, it was likely the first medication dispensed by practitioners of the healing arts. Spiritual ritual and medical practice were intertwined, with wine occupying a central position in the liturgy of both. Though the priesthood and the medical fraternities eventually diverged, their roots trace back to the grapevine. Wine became a sacramental symbol and a practical medication, a vehicle for commerce and a conduit for diplomacy and ceremony; it was without doubt the original celebratory libation, and has always been considered nutrition for the soul as well as a lubricant for the heart. It is fair to propose that wine made civilization possible, given the host of health and social problems that emerged when humans transitioned from nomadic hunter-gatherers to sessile lifestyles, and the salutary effects of wine in easing them. Even the enlightened concept of democratic government, an idea fermented in the Socratic symposia of the Classical Age, attributes to wine: *symposium* derives from the words "to drink together." Plato further makes the case by referring to wine as a "pharmakon," meaning a healing medicine.

Modern methods of archeology reveal that as soon as humans became able to make pottery vessels, they used them to store wine. Excavations in what is now Iran, in the area known as the cradle of civilization, have revealed signs of winemaking more than 5000 years ago. Sophisticated molecular analysis on scrapings of residue from a pottery vessel unearthed at an archeological dig at a site called Godin Tepe confirmed the presence of wine. Similar evidence of viticulture from another site, Hajji Firuz, indicates that wine was made as early as 5000 years B.C.* It is interesting to note that the wild Eurasian grapevine that is the ancestor of all modern vines for wine (*Vitis vinifera*) also appears to have originated in this area. Another relatively new science, paleobotany, has revealed evidence that these vines were cultivated and tended.

---

* In addition to certain compounds such as tartaric acid known to come from grapes, a tree resin called retsin, used to preserve wine and make pottery vessels more watertight, was also found. The practice of adding retsin to preserve wine continued for millennia, and in fact to this day in the form of a retsinated Greek wine called *retsina*. Other contextual evidence demonstrates that these vessels were used for wine and not grape juice, which would have quickly fermented to wine anyway. Most wines today use sulfur compounds for preservation.

Cultivating a healthy interest in wine

The ancient Greeks considered wine to be, quite literally, a gift from the gods. Dionysus (Bacchus in later Roman mythology) was the bearer of the gift and the one responsible for revealing its myriad aspects to the world. A cult of wine developed around Dionysus and his entourage, much as "cult wines" today are celebrated for their rarity and have dedicated followers. Often associated more with revelry and debauchery, the role of Dionysus is oversimplified and often misunderstood however, much like the question of healthy drinking in modern times. He may have been the original "party animal," but his gift of wine to the mortal world was considered a blessing. The word "wine" comes from the original gift of a grapevine from Dionysus to King *Oeneos*, (hence the term *oenology* for winemaking) in gratitude for hospitality. The very word for this luminous libation derives from the better parts of human nature.

> *Where there is no wine, love perishes, and everything else that is pleasant to man.*
>
> —Euripides, *The Bacchae*

In wine the condition of mankind was elevated, and through this the idea of theater was believed to have been bestowed by the gods upon the world. The life and adventures of Dionysus were the inspiration for the *dithyramb*, the satyr play, and a grand annual festival known as the Great Dionysia was held for centuries. The central event was a contest of poetry and theatrical works of comedy and tragedy. Because theater is both a diversion from, and a reflection of the human condition, its seminal purpose was to enlighten the mortal world about wine's hazards as well as its benefits. The original dyad of comedy and tragedy, symbolized by the two iconic masks of theater, reflects the dual aspects of wine: Dionysus used the vehicle of theater to demonstrate that while moderate consumption was joyful and liberating (comedy), excess could lead to tragedy. Classical Greek literature also refers often to wine as "nectar," which is thought to have derived from words meaning "to escape death." Wine, then, was endowed at its birth as both a divine substance and an anti-aging tonic.

The central role of wine in religious ritual and health practices was by no means limited to classic mythology. Theological texts of many faiths, including several prominent today, incorporate wine in fundamental ways. In the biblical great flood epic, one of Noah's first priorities after making landfall was to plant a grapevine for wine.[*] The Bible goes on to mention wine some 650 times, underscoring its importance during biblical times. The first miracle of Jesus is said to have been turning water into wine, (as opposed to beer, or grape juice for that matter), and apparently high quality wine at that. Wine as a proxy for the blood of Christ remains the basis for Christian sacraments.

Wine was the purview of divine beings from a variety of cultures, from the Sumerian goddess *Siduri* and the Egyptian goddess *Sekhmet (Hathor)*, to the Chinese deity *Ssu-ma Hsiang-ju*. A sixth century B.C. Indian medical text endorses the beneficial effects of wine, and predictably their pantheon also included a goddess for wine, *Sura*. In Japanese mythology, there is *Sukuna Hikona no Mikoto*, the god of medicine and wine (though the wine would have been sake, not grape wine, nevertheless illustrating a linkage between wine and health.) But despite its status in the spiritual realm, the dual role of wine as a curse and a blessing continued to be a conundrum both for religious institutions and health policy advocates throughout history.

By the third millennium B.C., winemaking had spread to Egypt, primarily under royal ownership and patronage. Wine was mainly an elite beverage, with beer being the libation of the working classes. But wine was more than a ceremonial draft; it appears to have been used as a treatment for asthma and a variety of other afflictions. Wine's position spanned across both spiritual and mortal life; Osiris, the Egyptian god associated with resurrection and fertility, is referred to in classical texts as the "lord of wine" during the annual Nile flooding known as the inundation, which restored and irrigated the farmlands. Wine symbolized rebirth and renewal.

---

[*] There is of course the matter of Noah's overindulgence on the occasion of the first vintage, a source of consternation on the part of his teetotaler son Canaan, resulting in the latter's banishment. Noah went on to live some 350 years.

Eventually the use of wine became more widespread, and Egyptian soldiers were known to have carried rations of wine. It was the Greeks, however, who first fully integrated wine into all levels of social, commercial, and cultural life. The Greeks brought wine and winemaking, along with new ideas such as democracy, to an expansive trading empire. Wrecks of ships from this period laden with wine amphorae containing as much as 300,000 liters litter the Mediterranean seabed. The importance of wine in the spread of ideals and quality of life during this period is paramount; trading in wine meant trading in ideas.

The role of wine in medicine became firmly embedded in Greek thought, spreading later to Rome and its dominion. Hippocrates (439-377 B.C.), known as the father of western medical philosophy, wrote at length about the properties of wine in medical practice. Of particular emphasis was the usage of wine for digestive maladies. Hippocrates enumerated at length how different types of wine affected body systems, and brought competing "humors" into balance; though in light of modern science it must be admitted that his observations were naïve, however well-intentioned.

Roman legions, like the Egyptians, were provisioned with daily wine, perhaps fueling the expansion of the empire. Wine appreciation was adopted around the Mediterranean rim, and on the shoulders of the Roman Empire throughout Europe. Viticulture was introduced to Bordeaux in the first century A.D., and the adoption of Christianity reinforced the position of wine in civilized society. Beer was considered to be the drink of pagans and primitive peoples, while wine was the libation of the pious.

The decline of the Roman Empire resulted in an enhanced role of the Christian church in stewardship of the traditions of viticulture. Ownership of a great number of vineyards was transferred to monasteries, ostensibly for production of wine for Eucharistic purposes, but output far exceeded the amount needed for that limited application. Many bishops, notably Gregory of Langres who later became Saint Gregory, possessed substantial vineyard acreage. Monks were allotted a daily ration of wine, and Saint Benedict established that Benedictine monks who were ill were to be afforded a greater allocation. The connection between wine and health practices was also reinforced by this arrangement, as monks learned the apothecary arts along with winemaking, often preparing medicinal herbs by dissolving them in wine. The first officially published pharmacopoeia (*Dispensatorium*, by Valerius Cordus in Nuremberg in 1546) lists wine as an essential component of the therapeutic armamentarium.

> *Satisfy your hearts with food and wine, for therein is courage and strength.*
>
> —Homer, *The Iliad*

Wine rations during military operations continued right up until the twentieth century.* But while one can conjecture that it was employed to stoke the fires of combat, or to alleviate the boredom or tension of a military deployment, its original purpose was more practical. Considering the poor state of sanitation in the classical world, and lack of understanding of the nature of water-borne illnesses such as cholera, the use of wine to decontaminate drinking water and to counteract pathogens from spoiled food was certainly an advantage both in military exploits and daily life. Clean drinking water would have been all but impossible to guarantee even if its importance were appreciated, especially during long campaigns. When Louis Pasteur called wine "the most healthful and hygenic of beverages" he was recognizing its important antibacterial properties, especially in the pre-pasteurization era. (Pasteur also described the science of fermentation, demonstrating that yeast breaks down sugar into alcohol, and bacteria lead to spoilage.) Alcohol and wine polyphenols are in fact excellent natural preservatives and antimicrobial agents, and studies have demonstrated wine's activity against the bugs that cause many food-borne illnesses, including *Salmonella* and *E. coli*. Some have even suggested making a wine-based disinfectant kitchen spray.

---

*   French soldiers deployed along the Maginot line were allotted up to a liter or more of wine per day, a closely guarded military secret. While one might conjecture that this contributed to the porosity of the defensive formation against the rapid advance of the Germans, wine was to play a vital role throughout the war, particularly in the resistance.

Out to Pasteur

It would be difficult to overestimate the contributions of the French chemist Louis Pasteur (1822-1895) to wine and health. His study of tartaric acid crystals (from wine) led to an expanded understanding of physical chemistry, but he is best known for figuring out exactly how fermentation occurs, how to control it, and how to prevent spoilage. It seems hard to believe that prior to Pasteur's work the whole process was essentially a mystery. He is of course best known for demonstrating that food spoilage could be prevented by heating (thereby killing the microbes that cause it), but a lesser-known fact is his insight that surgical wound infections are also the result of bacterial proliferation. This inspired the British surgeon Joseph Lister (immortalized in the name of a well-known antiseptic mouthwash) to develop the practice of surgical antisepsis, dramatically lowering mortality rates. Prior to that, surgery was a macho, dirty business, and if a patient was lucky enough to survive the procedure itself, a postoperative wound infection would likely finish them off. The idea of sterile technique was nevertheless considered to be more of an affectation and was slow to be accepted. But every successful surgical outcome today owes a tribute to Pasteur, and so at least indirectly, to wine.

Pasteur's work marks a milestone not just in the understanding of the biology of wine, but also in the emergence of modern medical science. Concepts of disease during archaic and medieval times were based more on superstition than rational deduction. Writers on health tended to focus on balancing the body's various fluids such as bile, phlegm, and blood, and adjusting the "hot" and "cold" elements; wine was a "hot" force, presumably so designated because of the sensation resulting from dilation of peripheral blood vessels. For centuries wine was purported to strengthen the blood, probably for the simple reason of its similar appearance. The empirical observation that adding wine to water made it safer to drink was likely the result of attempts to improve its drinkability more than application of hygenic theory.

Portable potability

Since the problem of potable water applied even more acutely on long sea voyages, the significance of wine in facilitating seafaring exploration cannot be overestimated. The pilgrim ships to America carried substantial cargos of wine. In fact, records show that much more wine than water was on board, as much as ten thousand gallons per ship.

An Australian conviction for wine

Like all seafaring enterprises of the time, the convict ships from Britain to Australia relied on wine in order to keep crew and passengers healthy and able to survive the long and grueling journey. In one instance (the 1814 voyage of the *Surrey*), a misguided captain and officers were found to have withheld wine rations from their convict passengers, to the tune of some 240 gallons. The result was a typhus outbreak that caused the deaths of a third of all on board, including many of the crew and officers, and even the captain. Reforms were subsequently enacted requiring ships' doctors to oversee and enforce the distribution of wine on board. Many of these jobs were taken by Royal Navy surgeons in search of employment after the Napoleonic wars. Eventually a large number of these physicians retired to Australia and founded wineries. It has been claimed that the majority of Australia's wine production to this day can trace its origins to wineries established by physicians. (Aficionados of Australian wines will surely recognize the legacies of Dr. Henry Lindeman (scion of the Lindeman wine company), and Dr. Christopher Penfolds, who established a medical practice in the 1840's at his estate, which he planted with vines and called the Grange.)

Although Puritanism came to be associated with Christian temperance movements in the nineteenth century, wine was a healthy part of the Puritan lifestyle. One prominent preacher, Increase Mather, referred to wine as "a good creature of God." Attempts to cultivate grapevines in the New World were given a high priority, with limited success, notably by Thomas Jefferson. Laws were even passed in colonial Virginia requiring settlers to plant vines and learn winemaking, and expensive consultants were brought over from France.

Despite the healthy mind-set about wine that characterized the Puritan ethic, attitudes soured during the nineteenth century. Gradually the distinction between wine—considered a temperate and even holy beverage—and distilled spirits eroded. The integration of wine with meals loosened, perhaps due in part to the rapid westward expansion of America and its continuing difficulties with attempts at viticulture, while such traditions in Europe became increasingly well-rooted. Wine was still a relatively uncommon commodity in the U.S., available primarily to the well-heeled; distilled spirits were much more suitable to a rapidly evolving, more mobile, and increasingly urban population.

Temperance activists initially made a clear distinction, with the Women's Christian Temperance Union, for example, advocating against distilled spirits but supporting moderate use of wine and beer. Alcoholism was recognized as a disease by the Swedish physician Magnus Huff in 1849, reinforcing the distinction between healthy drinking and abuse. But in the American way of thinking, the fallacy of extremes came to bear: If too much is bad, then any at all is bad. (The reverse also applies: If a little bit is good, then a lot is better; equally fallacious.) Laws banning alcohol were passed by a dozen states beginning in 1851. Under the banner of the "Anti-Saloon League", temperance movements were overtaken by prohibitionists, who not only pointed out the very real dangers of alcohol, but supplemented them with sometimes outlandish claims such as the risk of spontaneous combustion from alcohol consumption. Pamphlets included depictions of flames bursting from various areas of the bodies of unfortunate imbibers, along with vivid descriptions of their burned out corpses.

A nation carried away

Every drama has its hero and its villain, but in the case of Prohibition the former turned out in the end to be the latter. An immensely sour and misguided woman by the name of Carrie A. Nation was the spearhead of the movement, though it was the working end of a hatchet that she became known for. Believing she was on a mission from God, she would stage what she called "hatchetations" which involved violently attacking saloons and hacking away at barrels of whiskey. She even hired a manager, changed the spelling of her name to "Carry A. Nation" and trademarked it, went on tour, and peddled her own "Famous and Original Barroom Smashers" so that her followers could spread the goodwill in her wake.

Her world view was spelled out in a 1905 paean, *The Use and Need of the Life of Carry A. Nation,* in which she blessed her readers with diatribes on everything from morality and race relations to a particularly paranoid conspiracy theory involving Masons, as well as of course food and alcohol. She held particular enmity for foreign foods and wine. All this was based on a resurrection of naïve medieval concepts of food being classified as either a "flesh former" or a "body warmer" and alcohol being neither. She went to great lengths to promote this theory and to specifically discount any notion of wine as a food. What the country really needed and could have used was a more rational and sober discourse, if you ask me.

The prohibition movements reached a crest around the turn of the century, and swept across the country. Europeans, meanwhile, had their own issues with alcohol but continued to perceive wine in the context of healthy living; in 1903 the French Parliament, following Pasteur's proclamation of a few decades earlier, officially declared wine to be "healthy and hygenic." Wine consumption was encouraged even by temperance organizations. In Britain, medical papers were published recommending the prescription of specific wines for specific ailments, though it seems unlikely that their rationale would stand up to modern scientific analysis. But the temperance trend in America continued toward strict abstinence. Interest in wine as medicine faded as pharmaceuticals such as aspirin were developed, and public sanitation programs improved water quality.

Wine is my doctor

From the late nineteenth through the early twentieth centuries, the wine industry in France had suffered tremendously, from the phylloxera devastation that wiped out the vineyards, the Franco-Prussian War, and the first World War, and as Americans were drying out under Prohibition, the French were eager to celebrate renewal. This spirit was embodied in some very entertaining if preposterous publications, notably the 1936 book *Mon Docteur, le Vin,* complete with watercolor illustrations by the well-known artist Raoul Dufy. The book imaginatively makes the case for wine as a cure for just about everything, with chapters how wine counters typhoid fever, nervous depression, appendicitis, obesity, and diabetes. Wine was indispensable for writers (sip), and necessary for artistes and athletes alike. (A recent publication demonstrated that resveratrol from red wine indeed improves athletic endurance!) Just as important, wine was purported to build moral character, and necessary for maintenance of *jeunesse et l'esthetique* (youthfulness and beauty) and aging gracefully.

The case had actually been made a few years earlier by a past president of the Academy of Medicine, a Doctor Alexandre Guéniot, with his 1931 book *Pour Vivre Cent Ans, ou L'Art de Prolonger Ses Jours* (How to live to be 100, or the art of prolonging one's years). Of course wine was a central part of the formula. (His recommendation? "Let us drink wine, good wine, natural wine, old wine if possible!") Dr. Guéniot could certainly write with authority on the subject of longevity, as he was 102 when the book was published, one year before his death.

By the time the 18th Amendment was passed in 1919, 33 of the then 48 U.S. states had already banned alcohol. The only exceptions were wine for religious and medicinal purposes, resulting in a sudden upsurge in these applications. But intolerance with drinking reached a zenith with the Nazi Party, which endorsed the sterilization of thousands of alcoholics as part of its eugenics program. (Conversely, control of the French wine business was among the chief aims of the German invasion, and massive quantities of wine were shipped to Germany during World War II.)

In America, the effects of Prohibition on attitudes about wine are difficult to gauge, but the resultant rise in bootlegging of poor-quality and even dangerous spirits, along with gangsterism and related violence may have introduced elements as harmful to society in general as alcohol abuse. It certainly disrupted any tendencies there may have been toward healthful practices of drinking wine with meals. In any case, the repeal of the 18th Amendment and the end of the war finally set the stage for a serious look at wine (and other alcoholic beverages) and health. But it would be nearly another half-century before we began to recognize just how profound wine's healthful properties are, and how sadly misguided public policy has been.

Wine ...is one of the staples of civilization

—Evelyn Waugh

Chapter 2

Science and Sensibility:
A Rational View of Anti Aging

Nothing is more useful than wine for strengthening the body, and also more detrimental to our pleasure if moderation is lacking.

—Pliny the Elder

Science and technology were ascendant throughout the twentieth century. Life expectancy doubled from the beginning of the century to the end (though now indications are that it is declining again in the new millennium due to poor dietary habits in developed nations). Economic expansion, public health measures, and improved medical technology led to improved quality of life by many measures. A population explosion was spurred on not only by the mid-century burst in birth rates, but by the fact that people could reasonably expect to live longer and more productively. And as the population grayed, interest in anti-aging naturally intensified.

But even as the birth of the twentieth century was known for quackery and traveling "snake oil" salesmen, an expanding anti-aging industry emerged a hundred years later with an only vaguely firmer rooting in science. Because of this, anti-aging as a scientific discipline has had a credibility problem, but it is an emerging understanding of wine biochemistry that has skeptics paying serious attention and the research community abuzz. It is fair to say that the field has been re-energized, and what was recently all but ignored is now the subject of many hundreds of scientific publications annually, and the pace is accelerating. It is a wine-derived compound—resveratrol—that appears to have unlocked one of nature's biggest secrets, by showing that significant extension of lifespan may be achievable.

Plastic surgeons are on the front lines of the anti-aging battlefield. Every day I see patients who might say something like "I just want to look as young as I feel." As a result of healthier attitudes, and safer, less invasive techniques, the social stigma of having cosmetic procedures for restoration of a youthful appearance is largely a thing of the past. Patients consider cosmetic plastic surgery more of a maintenance ritual, and a focus on better nutrition, exercise, and healthful lifestyles now seems less out of phase with the occasional lift and tuck. Not that there is anything unhealthy about all of that, and indeed plastic surgery can be a wonderful thing: plastic surgeons heal the wounded, restore hope and well-being to the disfigured, and help those who want to enhance the visible benefits of healthy living. But the plastic surgeon is ultimately an illusionist when it comes to the question of biological aging. We would also like to be able to help our patients who say, "I just want to feel as young as I look!"

Interest accrues with age

Interest in anti-aging has certainly intensified as populations in developed nations have matured.* On the cover of their October 22, 2003 edition, the magazine of the AARP (American Association of Retired Persons) declared "Sixty is the new thirty," underscoring how people can look forward to a longer and healthier life. The simple fact that we are living longer begs the question of what the realistic upper limit of a vigorous and productive lifespan really is (some say as much

---

* The number of Americans over 65 has increased 10-fold over the past century. People older than 85 constitute the fastest-growing segment of the population, and the number of centenarians has been increasing by 7% per year since the 1950's.

as 150 years!). A massive industry has blossomed around the modern quest for the elixir of immortality, with Americans spending somewhere between $4 billion and $16 billion annually on everything from Ginkgo biloba pills to hormone shots. Herbal supplements and megavitamins have become the snake oil of the new era.

The difficult and painstaking work of real science all too often gets trampled in the rush to market with every new discovery. A 2002 Position Paper in *Scientific American* rang alarm bells about what they called "a disturbing and potentially dangerous trend" in the anti-aging industry. They bemoaned the "proliferation of health care providers and entrepreneurs who are promoting anti-aging products" with "little or no scientific basis." So my own process, as I surveyed the medical literature on anti-aging for this book, was to eliminate everything that wasn't rooted in legitimate research, and see what patterns emerged from what remained. What I discovered was that one of the most important keys to longevity and healthy living has been right under our noses—literally—the whole time.

Despite the growth of misleading come-ons and outright fraud in the anti-aging arena, enormous strides have been made in unlocking the mechanisms of aging on a fundamental biologic basis. It is this science upon which we must rely in order to answer the questions about wine, health, and anti-aging. The first order of business is to define objectively what anti-aging is, and then to be deliberate in our application of the scientific method. Did wine have anything to do with Jeanne Calment's incredible lifespan, or was she merely a statistical anomaly? If we hope to truly understand the secrets of longevity, and to be able to apply them to our advantage, an open-minded yet skeptical approach is called for. Indeed, that cautious and objective process is the essence of the scientific method.

One immediate problem is that there is no strict consensus within the scientific community about what anti-aging is. Science writer Ben Bova wrote, in his book *Immortality*: "The first immortal human beings are probably living among us today." A more mainstream and rational view is expressed by S. Jay Olshansky and Bruce A. Carnes of the Center on Aging at the University of Chicago: "… ingesting vitamins, minerals and antioxidants will not eliminate aging and disease…" and "taking any of the other remedies currently being peddled by the advocates of extreme longevity cannot stop, reverse, or eliminate aging." Immortality may seem an unlikely prospect, but wine-derived science does offer some tantalizing possibilities, so somewhere between the rosy and the cynical scenarios lies the path we will follow.

Making sense of senescence

Scientists who study aging are known as *gerontologists*, and they do agree on certain definitions which are important in any discussion about anti-aging. Strictly speaking, aging relates to changes associated with the passage of chronological time; "biological time" leads to what is called *senescence*, which more precisely describes the progressive and inevitable deterioration in bodily functions that occurs over the lifespan of a living organism. Since there is no known way to actually reverse time, anti-aging more correctly refers not simply to longer survival, but to enhanced wellness and overall quality of life. The currently popular term is "age management," an acknowledgement of the limitations of our present state of knowledge, at least in a clinical sense. But while we cannot literally turn back the clock (though plastic surgeons can make it appear that way), we can modify age-specific actuarial risk of death and disease, and in fact there are some powerful tools at our disposal.

A logical starting point is to take a systematic look at centenarians (those who live a hundred years or more) and try to discern what factors are associated with their extreme longevity. One obvious feature to consider is genetics; it has long been appreciated that in order to live long, one would do well to select ancestors with long lifespans. Not surprisingly, this observation is borne out to a degree by statistics, and specific genes have been identified that program for longevity. Scientists are still learning more about how these genes work.

But while heredity is obviously helpful, it doesn't go as far as one might think. If there is a sort of "longevity equation," genetics only provides the answer to about a third of the variables needed to solve it. (Jeanne Calment didn't come from a line of long-lived ancestors, and outlived her children.) Other factors—ones we can actually control—appear to be of greater consequence. Dietary and drinking habits, along with exercise and other lifestyle factors, are ultimately more important than genetic pedigree. So it would appear that that it is how one plays the cards that were dealt that wins the hand, encouraging news indeed.

Ponce de Leon and the Fountain of Youth

The poster boy for the search for the key to youth and longevity is *Ponce de Leon*, who traveled with Columbus on his second voyage, and later founded a colony on Puerto Rico in 1508. He became obsessed with a legend of the "Fountain of Youth" from local natives who described its location somewhere north of the island. All who bathed in or drank the waters would become young again. (It is possible that the local natives, unhappy with European rule, concocted the story as a ruse to lure him away from the island, while some speculate that he was motivated by his inability at age 55 to satisfy his much younger wife.) His quest led to the discovery of Florida, but not longevity. An interesting side note is that Florida later became the first state where wine was successfully made, by French Huguenots in the 1560's. Ponce de Leon may simply have been a few decades too early.

There are other behavioral considerations that gerontologists have identified as having measurable influence on longevity. The simple habit of keeping an active mind, seeking out challenges and new experiences seems to have an impact. (Jeanne Calment recorded a rap CD recounting her life's experiences at age 120; that had to have been a novel experience!) Volunteer work, ties to community and heritage, and an active social network are related aspects of a longevity strategy. It is not difficult to picture how wine, with its ability to bring people together with a sense of camaraderie and celebration, might dovetail with these other anti-aging behaviors. As we will see, there is substantial evidence for a strong association between regular wine consumption and other healthy habits, thereby magnifying whatever biochemical benefits it may have.

Suddenly senior

Yet regardless of one's genetic makeup and lifestyle, aging happens. Cells deteriorate, slow down their metabolism, and become senescent. There are several theories about how this occurs, and it is worthwhile to consider these various schools of thought so that we may better determine how wine chemistry might intervene.

Aging theories fall broadly into two categories, known as *programmed* theories and *error* theories. Subscribers to the former emphasize the importance of certain genes associated with aging, which are switched on and off according to a predetermined program. One manifestation of this, for example, is the observable decline in levels of certain hormones with advancing age. The gradual shutting down of the immune system may also be a pre-programmed "auto-destruct" sequence.

Although great strides are being made by the researchers who study the switches that comprise the operating system for our genetic code[*], others aren't willing to wait for a more comprehensive solution. "Age management" practitioners, noting the decline in many hormones with age, believe that the answer is a simple as boosting hormones back to youthful levels with injections and pills. Perhaps if we can trick our bodies into "thinking" they are younger with hormone supplements, aging will slow down (so the theory goes.) A popular example of this is growth hormone (which does a lot more than stimulate growth.) Users of growth hormone regain energy, muscle mass, and a number of other attributes of youthfulness. Other hormones in the anti-aging arsenal include testosterone, estrogen, and melatonin. (Substances in red wine also have hormone-like properties that have been shown to counteract osteoporosis and other degenerative conditions—more on that later.)

The problem is that no one can say for sure whether these declining hormone levels are an entirely bad thing, especially from an anti-aging point of view. It is perfectly plausible that the slower metabolism associated with ebbing hormones reduces "wear and tear" thereby

---

[*] DNA switches are controlled by a process called *methylation*; wine polyphenols have been shown to interact directly with DNA methylation enzymes.

affording a long-term survival *advantage*. It could well be argued that this makes more sense than ramping up senior citizens' hormone levels to teenager titers with the hope that they will live longer. Indeed, hormone manipulation carries known risks; with growth hormone, these include carpal tunnel syndrome, diabetes, and possibly increased odds of cancer. Furthermore, there is *no* published evidence to suggest that hormone supplements* increase lifespan.

Eos and Tithonus

Classical Greek mythology seems to have an allegory for everything, including anti-aging. The fable of Eos (Aurora in the later Roman pantheon) illustrates the importance of quality of life in the longevity formula. Eos, goddess of the dawn, was as beautiful as her position implied. She fell in love with the mortal Trojan prince Tithonus, an act that was perceived by her peers as a bit of a disgrace and not befitting her divine status. She pleaded with Zeus, pointing out *his* many dalliances (Dionysus was the offspring of Zeus and a mortal woman, and his wanderings were the result of banishment by the jealous Hera), so Zeus in turn granted Tithonus eternal life.

Unfortunately, eternal *youth* was not part of the package, and eventually Tithonus slipped into decrepitude, sustained only by the gods' ambrosia. Though Eos's love never waned, he eventually became so frail that he was locked away in a chamber whence his feeble cries could be heard. In time the gods took pity on him and changed him into a cicada. So be careful what you ask for!

---

* There is an ongoing semantic argument about where hormone *replacement* ends and hormone *supplementation* begins. Some practitioners recommend tweaking hormones only to age-adjusted norms, others to levels typical of early adulthood.

An intriguing offshoot of the genetic switch line of research may hold more promise. In response to certain types of stress, organisms adapt by activating genes that code for proteins with properties protective against stress-induced damage. These compounds are known as *heat shock proteins* because they were first identified in fruit flies exposed to a burst of heat. These proteins have now been identified in virtually every form of life, from plants to people, an indication of their fundamental biologic importance. Heat shock proteins are induced by a variety of stresses and have a range of interesting properties. These include, for example, the ability to attenuate injury to heart muscle during the oxygen deprivation of a heart attack. They appear also to help clear and repair damage to tissue after injury.

Researchers in aging have observed that the body's ability to manufacture heat shock proteins in response to stress recedes with age. But as we will see in more detail later, wine again enters the picture. A substantial body of evidence exists that heat shock proteins can be activated by substances in red wine, bypassing the stress stimulus—a win/win scenario if there ever was one. Heat shock protein activation is likely one of the reasons why wine drinkers not only have fewer heart attacks, but survive them better and have stronger hearts when they do.

Despite the intriguing possibilities that longevity genes imply, aging is a much more complex phenomenon and not subject to easy manipulation. The admittedly exciting prospect that we may someday be able to engineer our way to longer lives through genetic exploitation is ultimately only a partial answer. Cancer cells, for example, are able to divide and grow forever, but they eventually overtake and destroy the body. The control mechanism for genetic expression is a multilayered cipher without much margin for error, and so it seems unlikely we will be able to simply flip a few genetic switches to turn on longevity genes and expect it to work.

So while there is presumably some biologic *raison d'etre* for longevity genes, the *programmed* theory provides an unsatisfying explanation and offers an incomplete solution. We don't grow old and die simply because our genes tell us to, or get too "lazy" to make hormones or antibodies to fight disease. In the era before vaccines and modern health care technology, there wasn't much speculation on this subject because few lived long enough to die of "old age." But in developed countries now it is the *degenerative* diseases—heart disease, cancer, Alzheimer's and the like—that concern us. These diseases, which result from cumulative damage to cells and tissues, and most especially to the DNA in our genetic blueprint, represent the *error* theory. Errors in genetic transcription, mistakes in manufacture of vital proteins and enzymes, and slip-ups in a variety of metabolic processes result in overall deterioration. Longevity genes will do us little good if we are senile and crippled. Central to the error theory is *oxidative damage*, the presumptive cause of most of this degradation.

The INDY Race

The common fruit fly, *Drosophila melanogaster*, is a favorite subject for aging and genetics researchers. The relatively short lifespan of these insects allows for anti-aging interventions to be studied with statistical precision in large populations. The fruit fly genome has now been mapped in detail, and at least three "longevity genes" have been identified (these are actually mutations in genes that would normally limit lifespan.) One of these has been dubbed INDY for "I'm Not Dead Yet." Flies with these genes not only live much longer, but they are quite vigorous as well. By the time 90% of their peers were dead, these flies were still sexually active and reproducing. Interestingly, a similar effect has been found when normal fruit flies are fed the red wine extract *resveratrol*.

The Inflammation Age

Despite the vastness of the anti-aging battlefield and the multiple fronts of the war, hope persists for simple and unifying solution. We cling to the wish for a "silver bullet" that will annihilate the enemy in a swift and bloodless assault. A November 2003 Reader's Digest cover story titled "The new pill that can end aging" is emblematic of the crusade. Is victory really in sight?

The enemy combatants in the antioxidant war are the aptly named "free radicals". These molecular miscreants are an inescapable consequence of our dependence upon oxygen; animal metabolism is in essence a controlled burn, with toxic by-products just as with any other fuel-burning engine. Add this to the list of life's ironies: the most basic requirement for living—oxygen—may also hasten our demise. That is not to say that fresh air is a bad thing, but from a purely physiologic point of view it isn't an unmitigated blessing either.

How did we get into this pickle? Plants give off oxygen as a toxic by-product, while animal life, with much higher demands for energy, uses this oxygen to advantage, in order to fuel a faster rate of metabolic combustion. The result is a symbiotic relationship between the domains of animal and plant life, but it comes at a price for us: just as iron rusts and cut apples brown by simple exposure to oxygen, oxidative metabolism results in a certain degree of physiologic corrosion. The biological processes involved here are considerably more complex than that, but the analogy serves as a useful starting point.

Free radicals are produced from a number of sources in addition to being a by-product of oxidative metabolism. Among the more important is tobacco, as well as alcohol and a form of iron called *heme* (pronounced "heem"), the primary dietary source of which is red meat. Alcohol is another pro-oxidant. Some are manufactured by necessity by the body's own immune system.* White blood cells, the infantry of our defenses against attack by viruses, bacteria, and other pathogens, employ a toxic brew of oxidants as their primary weapon system. The invaders are neutralized by the oxidant onslaught, but the spent molecules spill out and release free radicals capable of damaging the host. Chronic infections and other conditions of accelerated immune activity such as arthritis are associated with higher degrees of oxidative damage for this reason. The result is a state of ongoing inflammation, with consequences throughout the body and most especially with aging. Hepatitis, for example, leads

---

* This begs the question of whether it is an entirely good thing to suppress oxidation. One oxidizing molecule, nitric oxide, helps nerve cells communicate and blood vessels to relax.

to a higher risk of liver cancer, likely due to chronic oxidative insult to liver cells.

The possibility that free radicals might play a role in the degenerative diseases that contribute to senescence has its roots in research as early as the 1920's. By the mid-1950's, the mechanisms by which oxidation contributes to cellular deterioration were being fleshed out in more detail, in particular by physician-chemist Denham

---

Eliminating free radicals

One of my favorite references to the free radical theory of aging is the 1983 James Bond movie, *Never Say Never Again*. It is the last one with Sean Connery as Bond, and the opening sequences incorporate his elder status into the story line by having the aging agent undergo a series of simulations to determine whether he is still fit to work in the field. As his performance is being critiqued by "M" the dialogue goes something like this:

M: "Too many free radicals, that's your problem."
Bond: "Free radicals, sir?"
M: "Yes, they're toxins, that destroy the body and the brain. Caused by eating too much red meat and white bread, and too many dry martinis."
Bond: Then I shall eliminate the white bread, sir."
After Bond is given a rehab assignment to get in shape, he exits and is asked by Moneypenney whether he has been given a mission.
Bond (conspiratorially): "Yes, Moneypenney. I'm to eliminate <u>all free radicals.</u>
Moneypenney: Ooh, do be careful James.

I don't know whether Sean Connery took the free radical theory to heart in his personal life, but in 1989 at age 60 he was named People Magazine's "sexiest man alive".

Harman at the Donner Laboratory of medical physics at the University of California at Berkeley. Much of the credit, though, is given to biochemist Bruce Ames, also at Berkeley. Ames used to be better known for an eponymous test that predicted whether a chemical could lead to damage to DNA and cancer. The "Ames test" is still widely used to identify potential carcinogens in everything from artificial sweeteners to house paint.

Ames became intrigued by the observation that free radical damage accumulates with age in direct parallel to the rise in cancer risk. He was the first to document that DNA oxidation increases with age; in rats, for example, there is twice the amount of oxidative damage at 2 years as in 2-month old subjects. He also observed that the faster an animal's metabolism, the more free radicals were produced, explaining the inverse relationship between metabolic rate and lifespan. Oxidative damage provides a convenient explanation for this relationship, since faster metabolism, with its higher oxygen consumption, results in higher production of free radicals. The tortoise, a symbol of longevity in many cultures, outlives the hare by well over a century, possibly because of the dramatic differences in their metabolic rates. (Keep that in mind if you are ever tempted to use "metabolism boosters.")

Unstable elements

Free radicals are named because they are so unstable and reactive. They careen recklessly around looking for trouble, and are capable of wreaking havoc throughout the biomolecular world. Ames implicated free radicals in an array of age-related diseases, including cancer, cardiovascular disease, immune-system decline, brain dysfunction, and cataracts. A review article in the medical journal *Preventive Cardiology* in 2003 observed that "Oxidative stress appears to be of fundamental relevance to diseases as diverse as cancer, atherosclerosis, and Alzheimer's disease." Another journal, *Mutation Research* noted that same year that "Free radicals play a crucial role in the pathophysiology of a broad spectrum of diseases ..." It is no exaggeration to say that one of the most significant medical discoveries of the late twentieth century is the recognition of inflammation as the trigger for cardiovascular and other degenerative diseases. Indeed, the terms "free radical" and "anti-oxidant" have become entrenched in the modern vernacular, and few seriously question the basic soundness of the theory. This may be in part because it suggests such a simple and logical means of countering it: Just take a vitamin!

Planting SOD

Of course it isn't quite that easy, but we are not completely defenseless against this molecular mayhem. An enzyme called *superoxide dismutase*, or SOD, converts free radicals into hydrogen peroxide, which is then further processed by another enzyme into water and oxygen. Generally, these systems are quite efficient, and some prominent anti-aging researchers have openly expressed skepticism about whether their function can be improved upon with antioxidant supplementation. A study with earthworms (another useful subject for aging research) provides some support for the theory of oxidative damage though. When the slippery subjects were immersed in a liquid containing a synthetic version of SOD, they lived up to 44% longer.* Fruit flies survived an extra 30% after they were genetically engineered by inserting extra copies of the SOD gene into their DNA. This implies that if we can find a sufficiently robust anti-oxidant, it should be able to make a meaningful difference. Conveniently, red wine's antioxidants provide a ready explanation for many of its benefits.

Free radical damage is relentless, though, and eventually the damage becomes too extensive to overcome regardless of how effective our front line defenses are. The most dangerous effects are on DNA, which must expose itself every time a section of the DNA helix unzips so that a gene can be accessed, which is pretty much all the time. (Conversely, the

---

* I haven't found any studies that simply added wine to the worms' diet, but there is at least one where they added alcohol to see how well it was absorbed. Apparently, they did indeed get drunk, though how one determines the "I love ya man" moment in the worm's behavioral repertoire is a mystery to me.

parts that are not being accessed must be kept tightly coiled, and this is done by proteins called histones; we will see later how wine-derived molecules help to stabilize this whole process.) The environment inside of a cell is analogous to the floor of the stock exchange, with "buy" and "sell" orders frantically being shouted by chemical messenger molecules, each transaction requiring transcription of a gene. Only it all happens unimaginably fast, and free radical molecules swarm about, wreaking havoc like so many Keystone Kops. Eventually mutations (errors) in the DNA accumulate, and it may only take a few critical mutations in one of the four trillion cells in the human body to start a cancer.

There are actually repair enzymes that patrol along the DNA looking for these injuries, snipping out the damaged segments and splicing in an unmolested copy. These mutations are called *oxidative lesions,* and their numbers reflect the overall level of what is called *oxidative stress.* Because the damaged segments are disposed of, the level of oxidative stress can be measured by determining the level of excreted segments of damaged DNA as they cycle through the enzyme repair system and are jettisoned into the urine. Picture it like a reel-to-reel film that gets scratched by dust particles as it cycles through the projector; the dust is the free radicals, and the repair system automatically recognizes the faulty segments, discards and replaces them. The overall level of damage can then be determined by how full the wastebasket is. This gives scientists a useful tool for evaluation of antioxidant therapies, in particular dietary experiments with red wine, vitamins, or foods believed to have antioxidant properties. (Red wine typically performs best in these studies.)

Oxidative damage is implicated in another manifestation of aging known as *protein crosslinking.* Errors in the assemblage of these proteins cause them to clump together, interfering with their ability to function and sometimes just getting in the way. These proteins eventually accumulate and begin to interfere with cellular functions. Collagen, for instance, is the "building block" for most tissues throughout the body, and crosslinking causes it to lose suppleness and become brittle. Everything from blood vessels to skin stiffens. Another example is an abnormal protein complex known as *beta-amyloid,* which accumulates in the brains of people with Alzheimer's disease. Fortunately, wine polyphenols appear to have some unique abilities to counteract this buildup, above and beyond their antioxidant actions.

Fallacies and pharmaceuticals

The growing acceptance of the oxidative theory of aging led to a focus on dietary antioxidants, with a special emphasis on the antioxidant vitamins: A, C, and E. This provided a convenient explanation for the observation that people with diets high in fruits and vegetables (e.g., the Mediterranean Diet) tended to have lower rates of cancer and cardiovascular disease. (These populations also tend to drink wine regularly, but this fact was not considered in the early studies.) Pharmaceutical companies rushed to boost the content of the antioxidant vitamins in their supplement pills, even breakfast cereal started to be laced with antioxidants. The possibility that rates of degenerative diseases could be lowered led to numerous studies and bold proclamations. Nobel laureate Linus Pauling popularized the concept that everything from the common cold to cancer could be curtailed by vitamin C. Clinical trials have not validated either hypothesis, however, though many still reach for the vitamin bottle at the first sign of a sniffle.

Dozens of studies evaluating antioxidant vitamin supplements were published in the 1980's and 90's. It takes an enormous effort (and a lot of money) to complete a study large enough and over a long enough period of time to have statistical significance. There are critical steps that must be taken in order to eliminate bias in the study design; there are numerous subtle ways in which the *desired* result, rather that the *objective* result, can be encouraged. The gold standard is called a *double blind, prospective, randomized* study. In this type of project, neither the study subjects nor the evaluators know who had a placebo and who had the real thing until after the data is gathered.

One such study on antioxidant vitamins was done by the Harvard Medical School from 1982 through 1995, involving 22,000 physicians as subjects. This very large-scale, 13-year long project was designed to provide a definitive answer to the question of antioxidant supplements and cancer prevention. Half of the subjects were given beta carotene (vitamin A) and half placebo. When the code was unsealed and the data tabulated, no differences in overall mortality, cancer, or heart disease were found, despite expectations that diets high in natural beta carotene—the orange pigment in carrots and yellow vegetables—would be protective.

The science of science

This book is based on scientific studies done by others. So who exactly are these scientists, and why should we believe them? Although most of us place great faith in what science has provided for us in terms of comfort, productivity, and health, it is probably reasonable to aver that many people don't really appreciate how the system works. The scientific method is one thing–a quest to objectively discern how things work in the natural world–but someone has to fund all of this poking about in laboratories, and there needs to be some way of ensuring its reliability. This in turn requires a relentless process of filtering out bias, which often works against our instincts and may at times produce results that are at odds with what we hope to find. But if the findings are to be useful they must be followed wherever they lead.

Generally, it is government agencies (for example, the National Institutes of Health) that issue grants to academic centers for specific lines of inquiry. The actual work is carried out by graduate students and their professors. Private entities–pharmaceutical or biotech companies, for example–may also sponsor research projects. In either case, findings are published in scientific or medical journals and undergo a process called *peer review*. This independent screening mechanism ensures that standards have been employed in order to validate that proper methods have been used. Regardless of the sponsor, researchers stake their reputations on their published findings and so fudged data or unreasonable speculation can be expected to precipitate career-threatening consequences.

Important findings are then typically taken up for verification with further experimentation by other research centers. But despite the vigorous expansion of worthwhile findings in the field of wine and health, government sponsorship usually dries up just when things get interesting. For this reason, much of the growth of our knowledge in recent years is thanks to studies done in Europe, Asia, and South America. So for instance a researcher at an American university may develop a new method of measuring oxidative stress, which can then be used by someone in Chile looking at the role of red wine in the diet, inspiring another in Italy to carry it further. (In 2008 I published a research paper on resveratrol, and since it came out I have been contacted by researchers from 15 different countries on four continents.) We can confidently apply their findings regardless of source because of the process of peer review and independent confirmation. For these reasons I have intentionally limited my source material to studies published in mainstream academic journals wherever possible.

Similar studies were done around the world, looking at vitamins A, E, and C. The consensus is that there is no effect on any of the diseases studied, including heart disease and cancer, or in overall survival. In fact, more recent studies are suggesting an *increase* in overall mortality with vitamin supplements. In any case, the inescapable conclusion is that antioxidant vitamins are a bust as far as longevity and degenerative diseases are concerned. This may partly be explained by the fact that we now know that vitamins are relatively weak antioxidants, and increasing doses of vitamins are associated with potentially severe side-effects. Wine, on the other hand, has extraordinarily potent antioxidants; one study showed that wine diluted 1000-fold was still a stronger antioxidant than vitamin E.*

---

* There are a number of different laboratory tests that can be used to measure the antioxidant capacity of a substance. Regardless of the type of test, red wine consistently scores much higher than the antioxidant vitamins.

Wine, antioxidants and the Mediterranean diet

Wine was hardly the first place that researchers looked to find dietary antioxidants. The revelation came only after long parallel paths of research eventually converged. While chemists such as Harmon and Ames were deciphering the role of free radicals in disease and aging, epidemiologists were on the track of the Mediterranean diet. The now classic Seven Countries Study, which found that even poor countries without access to modern health care had exceptional longevity and health, pointed to the role of vegetables and whole grains as key. When viewed in the light of the newly emerging oxidative damage theory, attention was directed to the antioxidant vitamins so abundant in the Mediterranean diet. It all seemed to fit together neatly, but the cause-effect assumption turned out to be erroneous. Only after decades of research and dozens of large clinical trials did it become clear that the vitamins were a relatively unimportant element in the Mediterranean diet lifestyle. In retrospect, it seems remarkable that it took so long to identify the fact that wine was such a key ingredient, having been there all along.

C the whole picture

The underlying question is why the natural dietary sources are so effective, but the purified vitamin supplements were not. It might be helpful to consider one of the earliest identified forms of vitamin deficiency, *scurvy*. Sailors on the long sea voyages of exploration were prone to scurvy, a condition caused by breakdown of collagen, because the enzyme that manufactures collagen requires help from vitamin C. It wasn't until 1753 that the cause was identified, when the Scottish physician James Lind wrote *"experience indeed sufficiently shows that as greens or fresh vegetables, with ripe fruits, are the best remedies for it, so they prove the best preservatives against it."* Limes, being a relatively nonperishable source of whatever the curative nutrient was, became associated with British seamen in particular, hence the nickname "limeys". Allocation of citrus fruit aboard sailing ships eventually became as important as the wine allocations that made water safe to drink.

Vitamin C was eventually isolated and its chemical structure delineated in the early twentieth century by the Hungarian Nobel prize-winner Albert Szent-Györgyi. When Guinea pigs were deprived of vitamin C, they developed scurvy, as one would predict. But interestingly, pure vitamin C couldn't completely reverse experimentally induced scurvy, just as it failed to fend off colds and cancer in later human trials. It was eventually determined that additional plant-derived compounds called *flavonoids* were required. These substances are not only important in fundamental ways such as aiding vitamin C in rebuilding collagen, they are much more potent antioxidants. And you should not be surprised to learn by now that red wine is one of nature's richest sources of flavonoids.

There was considerable debate for a time about whether flavonoids should be considered vitamins in their own right.* But there are some difficulties with this concept, in particular the fact that there are hundreds of flavonoids, and they are in turn a subset of a larger family of compounds called *polyphenols* (Chapter 5). Moreover, each vitamin must have an associated disease state that develops in its absence; life isn't possible without vitamins for extended periods. (In fact the word "vitamin" comes from "vital amine," underscoring its essential nature.) With flavonoids and other polyphenol antioxidants, specific disease states do not emerge, rather a generalized degradation of metabolic functions that threaten longevity and overall health.

The practical view is that aging is the result of both genetic expression (programmed events) and errors related to oxidative damage and chronic inflammation, fallout from our fast-lane metabolism. Likewise, no ultimate solution to the aging equation will be as simple as cleaving the Gordian knot; we really do need to untangle it a strand at a

---

* The cofactor required for vitamin C to be fully active was likely to be the flavonoid *hesperidin*, which Szent-Györgyi named "vitamin P."

time. If it is only a matter of switching certain genes on and off, then a genetic engineering approach would be the eventual answer. A variety of antioxidants are being developed that are much more robust than vitamin supplements (included in these would be the pill that stops aging of the Reader's Digest story), but that seems an unsatisfying answer in and of itself also. We will see how wine is able to attack on both of these fronts, in addition to some possibilities that are much more intriguing and probably ultimately more important.

Is wine a vitamin?

While there are some remarkable similarities between wine's health properties and vitamins, it does take some creative license to christen *vitamin W.* Some believe that high doses of vitamins are the key to their effective use as antioxidants, but the doses required are frankly absurd. In the proper doses, however, each is associated with remarkable properties: in the case of wine, this includes a lowered risk of a wide range of diseases.

Metabolically speaking, vitamins are what are called *cofactors.* That is, they are essentially catalysts that facilitate the function of certain enzymes, the protein molecules that function like assembly line workers in the body's metabolic factories. One way to look at it is like the oil in a car's engine—a certain amount is required for it to run smoothly. Too little and the engine seizes up, too much and it clogs up the system. Likewise, a little wine helps grease the metabolic machinery (as well as the spirit) and too much gums up the works.

The resveratrol revelation

There is one sure-fire way to prolong life, at least in laboratory animals. Since the 1930's, scientists have known that laboratory mice live up to 40% longer when their caloric intake is reduced by a similar percentage from what they would normally consume. They not only live longer but are healthier and more resistant to disease. This phenomenon, known as *caloric restriction,* has been confirmed in other animal models as well, and is being tested in primates. A small group of humans practice caloric restriction, but there are significant drawbacks to this approach (as if living in a state of perpetual hunger isn't enough.) In animals growth is stunted, muscle mass is lessened, and they are observed to be less physically active compared to their counterparts who dine *ad lib.* Few humans are willing to adhere to such an austere way of life.

In recent years the mechanism of caloric restriction's effects on longevity has been discovered. The search now is for some means to activate this effect without suffering continual starvation. As luck would have it, the key is a substance in red wine: resveratrol (pronounced "rez-**vehr**-a-trol"). The effect is related to activation of certain genes, which appear to be able to initiate the longevity effect without the starvation. If this does indeed prove to work, it will be one of the most profound discoveries in modern biology.

So even if we could choose our ancestors or learn how to flip all the right genetic switches, it seems clear from what is known so far that the things that we can do—what we eat and drink, exercising mind and body, and avoidance of destructive influences—will always be important. We will see how wine can help not only to foster these healthy habits, but also to lay out the basis for directions in research of possible biochemical anti-aging interventions. But given the confusion that reigns in the anti-aging marketplace, with its competing claims, commercial pressures, and the tantalizing nature of the quest for the fountain of youth, a deliberate and cautious strategy is needed.

Key to such an approach is an understanding of the scientific method. An important foundation to this is simple skepticism; no matter how elegant or convenient a potential answer or explanation might be, the scientist says "prove it." This type of attitude should really apply to just about every decision we make, at least where there is a presumption of some scientific basis. Any sensible person can learn to use it, by employing what I call the *skeptic's checklist.* For a notion to elevate its status and become useful information, generally all of the criteria in the list need to be fulfilled, or at least there ought to be no inconsistencies. If, for example, a study of a certain population finds a

---

The skeptic's checklist

The scientific method requires a healthy degree of skepticism, especially where lifestyle factors are concerned and most importantly when considering the effects of an alcoholic beverage such as wine. The most essential thing to bear in mind is that a single study is rarely meaningful. Central to the process is *independent confirmation*. Before a theory about anti-aging can be accepted and applied, it needs to meet several criteria:

— Is there epidemiologic evidence (population surveys showing a correlation)?
— Do studies of different types reach the same conclusion?
— Is there a plausible cause-and-effect explanation?
— Is there experimental evidence to support the theory?
— Is there evidence from clinical studies showing a measurable health benefit?

Of no value at all (scientifically speaking) are what are termed *anecdotal reports*. These are stories such as "My uncle drank wine every day and he died at age 40 from heart disease" or something to the opposite effect. Some ideas reach the public consciousness without anything more than anecdotal evidence. Classic examples are taking vitamin C or the herb Echinacea for lessening the frequency or severity of the common cold. Neither of these has come close to filling the above criteria, and the "placebo effect" applies: if you believe something might work, for some people it does, even if it is an inert sugar pill. An interesting contrast is the finding that wine polyphenols actually bind and inactivate several viruses, so you might be better off having a glass of wine.

---

correlation between wine intake and low incidence of heart disease, but other types of studies always find the opposite (say, heart attack patients are found also to be wine drinkers), then we can't say whether there is in fact any relationship one way or the other. Simple probability means that some studies will produce an aberrant result, regardless of how well the research was conducted.

When the checklist is applied to most of the popular anti-aging products and procedures available, we find that they fail to clear even one or two hurdles. Vitamin supplements are important for a lot of reasons, but there is scant evidence that beyond levels in a healthful diet they will help you live longer, prevent cancer or Alzheimer's or measurably improve quality of life for most. The same applies for herbal supplements, and many "natural cures" although there is an encouraging trend to bring some clinical science to bear. Wine, of course, is a natural product made from plants, but evidence for its use as an anti-aging strategy fulfills a legacy planted millenniums ago.

> *Wine cheers the sad, revives the old, inspires the young, makes weariness forget his toil, and fears her danger; opens a new world when this, the present, palls.*
>
> —Byron, *Don Juan*

Chapter 3

A Good Thing

It has long been recognized that the problems with alcohol relate not to the use of a bad thing, but to the abuse of a very good thing.

—Abraham Lincoln

Comedian Henny Youngman had a joke that went something like: "I read somewhere that drinking is bad for you, so I resolved to give up reading." The joke works because of the subtext that underlies this whole topic, namely that alcohol is something we know is bad, something a little bit naughty perhaps, and this wine-health thing is a convenient excuse for breaking the rules with a wink and a nod. Fortunately for us, there is now plenty of literature to inspire both reading and drinking, though many still wonder whether any advantage can truly be attributed to alcohol. A product I recently saw advertised as having "all the benefits of wine without the alcohol" epitomizes the problem: Who could imagine that *booze* might be an important element of a healthy diet?

This brings us to the central paradox that has framed the subject of wine and health from time immemorial: Is alcohol a really necessary or desirable component of the health equation? In scientific terms, since alcohol encourages oxidative injury, wouldn't the anti-aging solution be more elegant without it? Given the backdrop of the many ills alcohol brings upon society and individuals, one can hardly imagine a more delicate subject. But from a public health perspective we can no more afford to overlook the plus side than to ignore the negative. We will examine both in good measure, and find a few surprises along the way.

We do have a rich vein of data to mine on this subject. Studies on the effects of alcohol (and now wine in particular) are almost too numerous to tabulate, and significant new reports appear almost weekly. It should be acknowledged at the outset that some of these studies are contradictory and subject to interpretation in different ways. But taken as a whole, the balance of evidence indicates that alcohol is indeed a good thing in moderation.

In order to make sense of these studies, we employ the science of *epidemiology*. As the term implies, epidemiology uses techniques of statistical analysis to identify associations and patterns in the spread of disease: epidemics. It is these patterns that are important; they connect not only individual cause-effect relationships, but different types of information.

Epidemiology of Snow in London

The science of epidemiology can be traced back at least as far as 1854, when a British doctor named John Snow sought to identify the source of a cholera epidemic. He tried something that was not common practice at the time: he interviewed the victims in detail about their habits and daily routines. By doing this he learned that they had all gotten drinking water from the same well at least once, implicating the water from that well as the source of the disease, even though it appeared clear and tasted fine. This approach seems simplistic today, but given the comparatively primitive state of medical knowledge and practice in the mid-nineteenth century (the notion that germs cause disease had not yet been proposed), it was a quantum leap ahead of prevailing superstitions and beliefs about the causality and treatment of disease. The system that Dr. Snow developed also works in reverse: By looking at the habits of *healthy* people, we might also find that they drink the same thing—red wine!

When the science of epidemiology is applied to the complexities of modern life, the problems become considerably more tangled. Sniffing out the source of a cholera outbreak or a flu epidemic is elementary by comparison. With lifestyle factors such as amount and type of alcohol consumption, the patterns can be difficult to ascertain, for many reasons. It is extraordinarily challenging to measure such behaviors with precision. The study subjects may not report their drinking habits accurately, whether by intention or not. Furthermore, there are always what are called *confounding variables*, which in the case of cardiovascular disease (for example) include includes such factors as high blood pressure, diet, smoking, personality type, genetic predisposition, etc. The conclusions derived from such studies are only as good as the data on which they are based, which can be variable and incomplete, despite the best intentions of the researchers.

This is one reason why epidemiologic studies must be taken "with a grain of salt" until they are independently verified, as the scientific method requires. The larger the population on which the study is based, and the more additional studies there are confirming the results, the greater the fidelity of the inferences from such analyses. The hypothesis that alcohol has specific health benefits can only be convincingly demonstrated with studies of different design, involving different subjects, by different investigators, all converging at the same point.

It takes a bit of effort to peel back the layers of the onion and find the core of truth. By now most of us are "immune" to reports in the news about the latest risk factor for cancer, or heart disease, or some other dire consequence of everyday pleasures. Many of these are trumpeted on the news before they have been independently verified, making the task of assigning relevance even more difficult. Since we rarely seem to hear about them again, we learn to actively ignore them. They blend into the background noise of a society already choking on too much useless information.

Our ears perk up, however, when there is the occasional bit of good news about lifestyle and health. Can it really be true that something so enjoyable as a glass of wine with dinner is actually *good* for us? Perhaps we should at least celebrate the fact that epidemiologists are now directing some attention to such questions, now that patterns of disease transmission are better understood and effective remedies more available. But if these good news reports are to be integrated into modern lifestyle dogma, they must be viewed in context and subjected to the same scrutiny as the others. Science is not about searching only for the results one wants.

The Framingham Frame-up

Heart disease from coronary artery atherosclerosis remains the leading cause of death in the 45 and up age group, and overall cardiovascular disease (heart attack, stroke, etc.) is the primary cause of death and serious illness in the United States. By the mid-twentieth century, cardiovascular disease rates had escalated so much it was considered to be an epidemic. Although most of us are now familiar with the risk factors (high blood pressure, smoking, and so forth) almost nothing reliable was known about the root causes of this growing health problem at that time. Well into the twentieth century, in fact, alcohol consumption was considered to be a primary *cause* of coronary disease. But when the science of epidemiology was brought to bear on the subject, the results would radically change our understanding of the role of lifestyle factors in cardiovascular disease and ignite a controversy about alcohol that smolders to this day.

The now-famous statistical associations between lifestyle factors and many "degenerative" diseases such as coronary disease derive from a landmark study initiated in 1948 called the Framingham Heart Study. The National Heart Institute (now the National Heart, Lung, and Blood Institute) embarked on what remains one of the most ambitious health research projects ever, in order to identify the factors that contribute to cardiovascular disease. They enrolled more than 5000 residents of the town of Framingham, Massachusetts, between the ages of 30 and 62, with the intent of monitoring their health and daily routines over a long period of time, looking for correlations to heart disease. This population is still being studied, and in fact the project has been continued into the second and third generations. Over the first 50 years of the endeavor, more than 1000 scientific articles were published in medical journals detailing a wide variety of links between lifestyle factors and indicators of cardiovascular disease risk. The very concept of "risk factors" has now become a standard part of the medical curriculum as well as common knowledge.

In 1974, after the Framingham Heart Study had been in progress for more than 25 years, a report on the factors related to deaths from coronary disease was prepared. Few were expecting the data to reveal a strong *reduction* in the odds of dying from heart disease with moderate alcohol consumption. Prevailing wisdom was that the reverse would be the case. The American psyche just wasn't ready, and in many quarters there is still resistance to the concept of alcohol as a good thing. Unlike the tradition of wine as a food in Europe, in America the underpinnings of crime and corruption of the prohibition era defined the alcohol legacy.

Framingham Highlights

Some highlights of the Framingham data regarding the association of heart disease with specific factors include: cigarette smoking, 1960; cholesterol levels, and high blood pressure, 1961; and lack of regular exercise, and obesity in 1967. The study has been expanded to include risk factors for stroke, with most of the same relationships found to be of similar risk (not surprising since stroke is most often due to disease of the arteries to the brain, just as heart attack is due to disease of the coronary arteries that feed the heart muscle.) Psychosocial factors such as "type A" personality have since been added to the list. The concept of "good cholesterol" (high-density lipoprotein, or HDL) and "bad cholesterol" (low-density lipoprotein, LDL) has also been reported, from Framingham and other studies. And we all accept as gospel, even if we don't practice it, that breakfast is the most important meal of the day, again based on Framingham.

In fact, the findings came as such an unwelcome guest that when the senior staff at the National Institutes of Health (NIH) reviewed the data, they demanded that the authors remove it! The lead scientist who had analyzed the data and prepared the report, Dr. Carl Seltzer, revealed in 1997 that the NIH officials had notified him in writing that "An article which openly invites the encouragement of undertaking drinking with the implication of prevention of coronary heart disease would be scientifically misleading and socially undesirable in view of the major health problem of alcoholism that already exists in the country." Furthermore, they insisted on an article stating instead that the data showed "no significant relationship of alcohol intake to the incidence of coronary heart disease" which was of course contradictory to the statistical observations in which they placed so much faith where other factors were concerned.

While the concerns about alcoholism were defensible, this attempted obfuscation on the part of these leaders within the scientific community is disturbing. Scientists are generally more cautious, and one might have expected calls for independent confirmation and no rush to judgment, rather than a "head in the sand" posture. Unfortunately, it still appears that all too often public science policy is the product of the same sausage-making apparatus that defines the political process, and with the same dubious quality of ingredients. Facts are colored to fit policy rather than the other way around. Some 30 years after the findings regarding alcohol and heart disease, the official Framingham website still omits this fact, though it has since been widely confirmed. Ironically, it may very well have been the prohibition era that spawned the epidemic of heart disease which in turn triggered the Framingham study in the first place.

Part of the problem might have been that in 1974, alcoholism was still widely considered more of a social problem than a medical condition, even within the scientific community. Alcohol was considered to be an inherently corrosive agent, both socially and medically, and any potential health benefits were surely felt to be overshadowed by its well-known detriments. But gradually since then a more enlightened view of substance abuse has emerged, with the recognition of genetic markers and specific diagnostic traits. Alcohol isn't the *cause* of alcoholism any more than motor vehicles are the cause of driving accidents. There is a certain percentage of bad drivers who shouldn't be behind the wheel, and a proportion of the population that is susceptible to alcohol addiction and shouldn't drink. An additional number are prone to poor judgment and destructive behaviors from alcohol intoxication and other forms of substance abuse, but the vast majority is capable of healthful and moderate consumptions patterns, despite the absence of a supportive social policy.

But the problem of alcoholism and binge drinking hangs over our subject like the sword of Damocles;* one winemaker I know described this aspect of being in the wine business as like sleeping with a loaded gun. The frequent tasting and toasting that are a necessary part of making and marketing wine can easily and almost imperceptibly slip toward excess, regardless of one's predisposition. The repercussions of problem drinking, on society and individuals, are incalculable. Alcoholism actually runs opposite to healthy drinking in its effects on families, communities, and personal health.

And the trends in drinking patterns are not encouraging. Lacking a societal custom of healthy drinking such as wine with meals, the average drinker views alcohol as a legitimate but recreational drug (a concept that tends to be reinforced by advertisers.) Statistics confirm that binge drinking episodes among adults of all age groups have been on the increase for several years. Of course drinking for celebratory reasons can be quite appropriate at times, but drinking for the purpose of intoxication is always a risky business.

Certainly for alcoholics, the question of healthy drinking is like asking how much gasoline is a reasonable amount to pour on a house fire. It was certainly a helpful thing when alcoholism came to be defined not only as a medical condition, but a treatable if irreversible one. But problem drinking behaviors span a spectrum of conditions. On the one hand, there appears to be an organic element to alcoholism, as in

---

*   Damocles was a sycophant in the 4th-century B.C. court of King Dionysius (no relation to the demigod Dionysus) of Syracuse, then a part of the Grecian empire. The king was regarded as a tyrant, and filled his court with flatterers such as Damocles, who regularly complimented the king on his wealth, power, and luxurious life. Damocles quickly accepted the king's offer one day try out his life for a day. When he sat in the throne, Damocles noticed a sword hanging over his head suspended only by a horse hair, a metaphor for what life as a ruler was really like.

many cases there are distinctive alterations in brain chemistry. Some alcoholics are, in other words, sort of "hard wired" to respond differently to alcohol. For these people, there is probably no sensible choice other than abstinence. (That is not to say, however, that knowledge of wine polyphenols is useless for them, as there are alternative dietary sources.) But for many problem drinkers it is not a matter of neural circuitry as much as a social matrix that lacks a heritage of healthy drinking habits.

It wasn't always this way, and doesn't have to be. That the pilgrims' endorsement of a wine lifestyle seems progressive compared to modern attitudes shows how far from the garden we have wandered. Dr. Benjamin Rush, a signer of the Declaration of Independence, was an early advocate of temperance but made a clear distinction between wholesome drinking of wine and alcohol abuse. He was one of the first physicians to describe alcoholism as a distinct entity, characterized by an *uncontrollable* desire for alcohol, in 1784. But several developments led to the decline of the concept of temperance as a philosophy inclusive of moderate wine consumption. One of these was likely the increasing use of distilled spirits during the nineteenth century, as wine was still generally difficult to produce, obtain, and transport in an expanding America.

Foremost was the belief (now held to be inaccurate) that anyone who consumed alcohol was at risk for loss of control, as opposed to there being a subset of individuals with an inherent predisposition. But it makes no more sense to discourage alcohol consumption across the board because some have a problem with it than to protest against chocolate because some are overweight. In fact, the right kind of chocolate consumption should be encouraged, like red wine, for reasons we will explore in due course.

So how did it come to be that alcohol emerged as a positive factor in the health equation? Perhaps the answer is buried deep in human development. We are equipped with an enzyme, alcohol dehydrogenase, the sole purpose of which is to metabolize alcohol. Regardless of one's belief about human origins, we seem designed to drink (either our genome was divinely designed for it or it emerged as an evolutionary response to an environmental opportunity.) For much of human existence, alcohol was a regular component of the diet, in the form of relatively low-concentration beverages: beer and wine. Distilled libations, with their much more potent punch, presented a distinctly new metabolic challenge. Not that I would object to the occasional single malt, but I would guess that problem drinking among those who stick with wine at meals is comparatively uncommon.

> *The dipsomaniac and the abstainer both make the same mistake:*
> *they both regard wine as a drug and not a drink.*
> —G.K. Chesterton

History shows us another thing, namely the folly of prohibition. It failed both as a social experiment and a health policy. A whole new category of violent crime emerged, and a tide of unhealthy Americans followed. Looking back, the Framingham data about alcohol and heart disease shouldn't have come as a particular surprise. In fact, studies from as early as 1904 provided a clear indication that alcohol had a protective effect against coronary disease. One such study, from a series of autopsies, found that atherosclerosis was uncommon in alcoholics. Several studies published in the 1950's and early 1960's reached a similar conclusion. In these studies, however, the only measure of alcohol *consumption* was alcoho*lism*, hardly a recommended alternative to coronary disease. Either way, a premature death is the result, with the notable difference being the fallout on society of alcohol abuse.

So although the door had been opened by the "unexpected" Framingham data, another two decades would pass before the data became massive enough to be discerned through the opacity of preconception. Dozens of studies have consistently confirmed and clarified the Framingham results, and extended them to conditions other than heart disease. We can now say with confidence that in the aggregate, the overall risk of death from all causes is significantly lower in *moderate* drinkers as compared to abstainers and to heavy drinkers.

The J-shaped curve

A pattern of regular alcohol consumption, then, appears to fulfill the first criterion of the skeptic's checklist: Multiple population studies paint a clear picture. This is a critical hurdle, since it would not be tenable to pursue the question of health benefits from alcohol without solid footing, any more than to prejudge them to the contrary. If one starts from a position of wine appreciation as a lifestyle preference, as I tend to do, then there is always the risk of unconscious bias in the interpretation of research reports. If we want the studies to validate our choices, it is ultimately untenable to embrace the reported health effects unskeptically. Studies revealing less salutary effects of drinking might be conveniently if not intentionally overlooked. But to do so would be to repeat the same type of mistake that the NIH scientists made in attempting to suppress the Framingham data.

In view of the reports on alcohol and health throughout the twentieth century, the Framingham data should have been considered a *confirmatory* report rather than a revolutionary and aberrant finding. But relentless questioning is what drives the scientific process, and it will be important to clear the remaining hurdles of the skeptic's checklist. While the data appears convincing, we need to see if the picture looks the same viewed from different angles. And we know that statistics, even from well-designed studies, are subject to manipulation and different interpretations; public relations professionals and marketers have made an art form out of the massage of statistics.

The skeptic's checklist reminds us that we need to determine whether different *types* of studies reach similar conclusions. In epidemiology, the relevant categories are called *population* or *ecologic* studies, *case-control* studies, and *cohort* studies (e.g., Framingham). If a consistent pattern emerges from a survey of these various studies, then we will look for *clinical* information, to test whether the findings can be applied in order to produce the predicted result. For example, does the addition of moderate amounts of alcohol to the diet of previous abstainers change their risk profiles in a measurable way?

Other questions researchers would ask are things like: How strong is the statistical association, and how specific is it? Is it dose-related? Is it independent from potentially confounding variables? And if there is a link between alcohol (and specifically wine) in the diet and lowered risk of a particular disease, exactly what is it that happens physiologically to produce this result?

The studies that followed the 1974 Framingham report clarified the picture further. Framingham and its progeny are *cohort* studies, that is, they track a population of specific individuals—the cohort—over time, looking for factors associated with different outcomes. Admittedly, it is a bit of a slog to plow through all of these studies, but that is sort of the point: there are a lot of them, they are large scale, and consistent across a variety of subject groups. One highly regarded survey is the Honolulu Heart Study, which tracked 7705 men of Japanese ancestry living in Hawaii. The 10-year follow-up was published in 1984, which again demonstrated a significant inverse relationship between alcohol consumption and heart attacks. The pattern that emerges from these studies isn't a linear one, however; although moderate drinkers fare better than nondrinkers, heavy drinkers fare worse. This holds true for both heart disease and overall mortality. When plotting mortality or disease incidence against alcohol consumption, the result is what is called the "J-shaped curve."

Several other cohort studies reinforce the concept of the J-shaped curve. One such study involved a prospective analysis of approximately

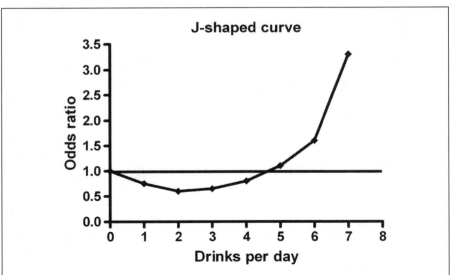

A typical J-shaped curve for cardiovascular disease. Note that the risk is the same for nondrinkers as for heavy drinkers, and about a 40% lower risk at 2-3 drinks per day.

1900 male employees of the Western Electric Company in Chicago. They were between 40 and 55 years old when enrolled into the cohort in 1957, and tracked for 17 years. In this group, the lowest incidence of heart disease was found in those who consumed an average of 4-5 drinks per day, with rapidly rising rates above that.

One of the leading early researchers in the field of alcohol and health is Arthur Klatsky of the Kaiser-Permanente health plan that started in California. Kaiser was among the first employer-based HMO-type plans (if not the first), which provided Klatsky with a defined population group from which epidemiologic data could be gleaned. (Since "health maintenance" is the ostensible purpose of HMO's, this type of data gathering is central to their mission.) After 10 years of monitoring, a plot of daily alcohol consumption habits against mortality from coronary disease once again produced a J-shaped curve. In 1997, a review of 129,000 hospital admissions for coronary disease reinforced the concept of the J-curve. Studies with similar results have been published between 1980 and 1983 from Great Britain, Australia, Yugoslavia, Puerto Rico, and Finland, confirming that the relationship applies to various populations and ethnic groups.

One critical point with these types of studies is the importance of discerning how much of the observed effect is due to alcohol, and how much to behavioral factors associated with alcohol. If, for example, moderate drinkers also tend to be nonsmokers, the lowered risk might be attributable mostly to that, with alcohol as a "marker" for it. There are, however, statistical tools that enable epidemiologists to sort these things out, and the pattern emerges in high relief: nonsmoking moderate drinkers still fare better than nonsmoking teetotalers. This holds up as well for other variables such as age, gender, blood pressure, and so forth.

Despite the impressive array of cohort studies attesting to the benefits of moderate drinking, our skeptic's lens requires that we look at the question from a different angle. So we turn to another type of analysis, the *case-control* study. This is essentially a review looking at cases with a specific diagnosis (for instance, hospital admissions for heart attack) compared to a matching "control" group with similar other characteristics. A typical study might compare patients admitted for the first time with a nonfatal heart attack to patients of similar age, weight, gender, and so forth, admitted for something unrelated to heart disease. Contrasting the two populations for alcohol consumption, for example, yields what is termed *relative risk* (the vertical axis on the J-curve diagram.) A number less than one correlates to lower risk.

At least eight case-control studies dealing with alcohol intake and cardiac disease were published between 1976 and 1985. Where the moderate-drinking subset was looked at separately (as opposed to the less useful question of simply drinking vs. non-drinking) a relative risk of 0.6 to 0.7 was found, or a 30-40% lowered odds of heart disease. The relative risk numbers shift to the upside of 1 with heavy drinking, again reinforcing the concept of the J-curve of the cohort studies.

Of perhaps greater importance is another study from 1982 (and confirmed subsequently) that looked at *patterns* of alcohol consumption as opposed to overall drinking. This study of coronary disease patients stratified them as regular drinkers, occasional drinkers, and non-drinkers. Significantly lower numbers of coronary occlusions were found in the patients who had consistently regular drinking habits; those who consumed more erratically were similar to non-drinkers. So you can't have a bottle of wine on Friday night to get the benefit of a glass a day, and one can easily imagine why those with more erratic drinking patterns might have other unhealthy behaviors as well, which would be expected to amplify the effect.

The J-shaped curve is now known to apply not just to cardiac disease specifically, but to overall mortality and, as we will see, other conditions such as cancer. Overall risk of dying is lower in those who regularly have 2 or 3 drinks, and higher in heavy imbibers. Excessive drinking can in fact be a cause of heart disease and stroke, and may be responsible for a form of chronic injury to heart muscle called cardiomyopathy. High blood pressure may also result from too much alcohol, with secondarily increased risk of stroke and coronary problems. Alcohol is, as we have noted, toxic to brain cells in a direct way and may be a mild carcinogen. At high levels of consumption, the well-known problems of liver cirrhosis, pancreatitis, and behavioral aspects of alcoholism all interact to rapidly escalate risk with increasing imbibition. But with all these dangers, there must be something powerful at work to overpower them at moderate levels of drinking.

The appearance of the J-shaped curve from every corner of the earth underscores the general agreement among those familiar with the studies that alcohol lowers cardiovascular risk (though many mistakenly assume this is the primary benefit.) But the third and fourth criteria of the skeptic's checklist require a plausible explanation of how the effect is created, and supportive experimental work. With the alcohol question, we are looking for something independent from wine polyphenols; otherwise this would be a book about grape juice.

About half of the protective properties of alcohol are attributed to an increase in the level of HDL cholesterol. HDL (High-Density Lipoprotein) is known as the "good" cholesterol, since it acts to remove cholesterol from deposits on the arterial wall and transport it away. Many separate studies have observed the correlation between alcohol consumption and improved cholesterol profiles, and the effect is seen with all types of alcoholic beverages, not just wine. One important clue is what is called a "dose-response" relationship, in other words the higher the alcohol intake, the greater the increase in HDL (up to a point.) This type of picture strengthens the cause-effect supposition.

The other half of the alcohol advantage is not quite as clear, but probably relates mostly to inhibition of an enzyme system associated with blood clotting. These enzymes, known as COX-1 and COX-2, are involved in mediating a cascade of inflammatory processes, and the initial phases of blood clot formation. Since a blood clot, triggered by a cholesterol plaque, is the precipitating event of heart attacks and most strokes, inhibition of clot initiation would help prevent them. And because alcohol's effect on clotting lasts only a day or two, this partly explains why frequent, regular consumption is important. Of course one could also take a "baby" aspirin daily for the same reason, so the merit of this aspect of the alcohol equation is debated. Potential anti-inflammatory properties from COX inhibition are less well linked to alcohol, but may be determined to be more important.

Public and professional interest in these studies intensified as the reports accumulated, but there remained a need for some sense of consensus. The leadership of the American Heart Association was no doubt mindful of these considerations when they convened a Nutrition Committee to draft a Position Paper on Alcohol and Heart Disease. The policy was published in the medical journal *Circulation* in 1996. The authors noted that in the United States, approximately one hundred thousand excess deaths could be attributed to alcohol-related diseases annually. So while they acknowledged that moderate alcohol consumption has well-documented protective effects against heart disease, they stopped well short of endorsing the concept that physicians should recommend its use routinely. They did rightly express caution about misinterpreting the data to give encouragement to those who should not drink (anyone with alcoholism, a history of pancreatitis or liver disease, pregnant women, and those on medications that might interact.) The best they could do was to affirm that moderate consumption of alcohol "might be considered safe."

But let's take this a step further. We may reasonably assume that the figure of 100,000 excess annual deaths from alcohol-related problems is fairly accurate, so by implication if alcohol could effectively be banned, the death rate from those causes would be reduced by that amount. But we must keep in mind that most drinkers do so in moderation, even in America. This segment of the population would experience an *increase* in rates of fatal heart disease and stroke, in the range of 30-40%. This would result in numbers that dwarf the thousands of lives potentially saved by a program of abstinence. (Recall the surge in cardiovascular diseases that followed on the heels of Prohibition.)

Europe has its own "Framingham" known as the Copenhagen Heart Study. Their scientists extrapolated their data with a purely public health point of view, to see what the result would be if alcohol was restricted. Their conclusion was that the number of lives saved by introducing daily alcohol in moderate doses to previous nondrinkers would save nearly four times as many lives as if all heavy drinkers cut back. This is certainly consistent with the J-shaped curve. In the United States, this would project to an annual figure of several hundred thousand unnecessary deaths from not drinking.

Omega Factor

In 2008 an additional benefit of moderate alcohol consumption was identified. A multicenter European study (England, Belgium, and Italy) known as IMMIDET found that regular non-binge drinking (one drink a day for women, two for men) was associated with elevated blood levels of omega-3 fatty acids. These are of course the heart-healthy fats from salmon and certain other fish. No differences were noted between drinkers of beer, wine, or spirits, a finding which points to alcohol as the responsible agent, though wine drinkers tended to show a greater benefit. Exactly how this effect occurs remains to be fully understood, but the researchers suggest that it is a trigger effect of alcohol on metabolism of these compounds, known collectively as essential polyunsaturated fatty acids.

A separate study from France, published at about year earlier, first hinted at the connection between omega-3's and wine. This study was actually a randomized trial of a dietary compound called alpha-linolenic acid, the main plant source of omega-3's. The study subjects, who had coronary heart disease, were subdivided into groups according to their alcohol intake, with a progressive increase in omega-3's with increasing alcohol consumption. (Most of the drinking in this population was wine.)

R. Curtis Ellison, M.D., a Professor of Medicine and Public Health and the director of Boston University's Institute on Lifestyle and Health has long been one of the foremost exponents of the benefits of alcohol on health. Dr. Ellison wrote in *The Wine Spectator* in 1998 that, based upon data from the Framingham study, "…only stopping smoking would have a larger beneficial effect on heart disease than for a non-drinker to begin having a drink or two each day." Not only does this place alcohol near the top of the healthy heart pyramid, but consider how difficult it is to get people to make permanent changes in the diet and exercise habits,

A down under view

One way to test the validity of the J-shaped curve, or any other statistical pattern, is to ask the opposite question: If moderate drinking is beneficial, what happens to moderate drinkers who change their drinking habits? A 2008 study from the University of Newcastle in Australia tackled this subject with a review of more than 13,000 women whose baseline health status was determined in 1996, then re-evaluated 8 years later, using standard markers of general health. As one would expect, the healthiest group was moderate drinkers; and not surprisingly, when moderate drinkers either increased or decreased their alcohol consumption, their health status declined. These types of studies are of course fraught with confounding variables, but the pattern held up even after adjustment for chronic medical conditions and other behaviors known to impact health. What is important to our case is that it confirms the pattern with independent and differently derived data, so the "bottoms up" view is the same as the top-down perspective.

to comply with taking their blood pressure pills, or to quit smoking. But how hard can it really be to think about having a glass of wine with dinner?

Improvements in cholesterol and blood coagulation, with their downstream benefits in cardiovascular risk are more than adequate justifications, but a fresh look at alcohol in a new light is revealing other positive attributes. In the main, health gains from alcohol are limited, with other constituents of wine being more significant; yet evidence has been put forth that arthritis sufferers may have reason to raise a toast. In early 2007, a report from the University of Göteborg in Sweden revealed that mice prone to rheumatoid arthritis experienced significantly fewer and less severe episodes when alcohol was added to their drinking water. The mice in the control group drank only water, while the fortunate ones in the treatment group had a 10% alcohol/water regimen. The findings were actually quite dramatic, with almost total abrogation of symptoms and pathologic findings in the alcohol group. No liver toxicity was found, as the dose was calculated to mimic what would be healthy moderate drinking in humans. Further, the researchers were able to demonstrate how the immune system was modulated to alter the inflammatory cascade of events that cause the arthritis.

In order to see whether this translated into a clinical effect, two case-control studies were done in Sweden and Denmark, and reported in 2008. The project reviewed 2750 people, about half of whom had rheumatoid arthritis, but otherwise matched for age, gender, etc. Subjects who reported drinking in the moderate range were 40-45% less likely to have arthritis, and heavy drinkers were more than 50% less likely. The biggest benefit was among people with known genetic predisposition to the disease, which implies a specific mechanism of action for alcohol in countering rheumatoid arthritis. So together with the data from animal studies, other population studies, and what is known about alcohol and cardiovascular disease, it becomes clear that we can't exclude alcohol as a player in the wine-health calculation.

Despite the historical reluctance on the part of the medical community and health policy makers to endorse the concept of a daily drink, the tide may be shifting, though public education on the subject still lags. The question remains how to circulate the good news without encouraging alcohol abuse. Even in France, the time-honored customs about wine are gradually being supplanted, and the new paradox might be why they are letting such a good thing slip away. In America, we are still groping for a sense of direction about alcohol, wine, and diet. For many, it will require a major change in the way we think, perhaps the very sort of mental challenge that helps us live longer too. Just don't look for a "recommended daily allowance" label on your wine bottle anytime soon.

"There are more old drunkards than old doctors."
— Benjamin Franklin

Chapter 4

The Most Healthful of Beverages

Wine can be considered with good reason as the most healthful and hygenic of beverages.

—Louis Pasteur

Despite continuing reluctance to embrace the idea that alcohol in moderation can indeed be a good thing as far as health is concerned, there is little debate in the informed scientific community. But this is a book about wine. What is it about wine that has not only inspired poets, philosophers, and lovers, but elevates it to special status in the health realm also? It isn't simply the alcohol, but it probably isn't the non-alcohol components in isolation either. The heart disease model again provides some insight, though it was really only the first step in a continuing journey of discovery.

Interest in research on the relationship of alcohol and health intensified after the CBS television show *60 Minutes* aired a feature in November 1991 called "The French Paradox." That now-iconic report disclosed that although the French should have higher rates of coronary disease than their American counterparts because they have higher dietary fat intake and smoke more, their mortality rate from coronary disease is only half. The presumed explanation was that the French drink more red wine, and in point of fact no better reason has been proposed since that time. The CBS report is largely credited with focusing attention on the question of whether wine in particular was the key, as opposed to alcohol in general.

Attention to the topic of lifestyle factors and heart disease is not as new as it might seem, even if the term "lifestyle" is a relatively modern construct. The "French paradox" was actually observed as early as 1819, when an Irish physician named Samuel Black, who was interested in heart disease, noted a high prevalence of cardiac symptoms in Ireland but a relative lack of emphasis on the condition among his French colleagues. He concluded that the difference was due to "the French habits and modes of living, coinciding with the benignity of their climate and the peculiar character of their moral affections." Unfortunately, the medical community practiced studious neglect of the subject for the next 160 years, when systematic epidemiologic data began to be published. Moral affections increasingly tilted toward a version of temperance that disdained all forms of alcohol, especially outside of central Europe, another paradox considering that heart disease was historically often *treated* with wine.[*]

But is wine the difference, or does alcohol from any source confer the same advantage? We have established that alcohol protects against heart disease, and in France wine is the primary delivery vehicle for alcohol. Indeed, throughout most of human history, wine was the alcoholic drink of convenience; distillation of spirits is a comparatively recent advent. (Beer may be almost as ancient as wine, but it is probably fair to say that *wine* is equivalent to *alcohol* in the historical sense. Beer in ancient times was considered to be a liquid form of bread.) And as I have mentioned, wine consumption may be a "marker" for other lifestyle factors, the French diet and smoking patterns notwithstanding. Wine drinkers do tend to be better educated, eat more vegetables, and exercise more. Could it be that wine drinkers are simply more sensible and relaxed, and healthier for it?

Though Dr. Black's observation of the French paradox in the nineteenth century was not widely appreciated, modern epidemiologists

---

[*] The original description of *angina pectoris* (chest pain characteristic of coronary disease) by William Heberden in 1786 noted that wine afforded "considerable relief."

began to note the pattern as early as the 1950's. The paradox exists between any country with high average wine consumption and others where beer or spirits are preferred. Finland, for example, has four times the heart disease rate of the French and the Italians, and much lower wine consumption. These types of comparisons provided some early clues that wine might be the essential difference.

> *Smooth out with wine the wrinkles of a furrowed brow.*
> —Horace, *Epistles*

The wine genie was finally uncorked in 1979 with the publication of a Welsh study comparing cardiac deaths to wine consumption in 20 European countries. Spurred by the mounting reports finding a "strong and specific association" between alcohol and reduction of heart disease, the researchers set out to examine the phenomenon with reference to *type* of alcoholic beverage and other factors. A remarkable and perhaps uncomfortable corollary finding was that the *negative* correlation of alcohol to heart attack deaths was stronger than the *positive* relationship of alcohol to road-accident deaths. This again highlights the thorny issues that arise when statistical methods are objectively applied to the alcohol question, because the clear implication is that *net* premature deaths would dramatically increase from a program of total abstinence.[*] These observations held true across all countries studied, regardless of variables such as access to health care.

Of interest to us is the next step the researchers took in their analysis, when they separated alcohol into its three main constituencies: wine, beer, and spirits drinkers. They found that by far wine had the strongest correlation. This linkage was in fact stronger than the positive correlation between high saturated fat intake and atherosclerosis, even more secure than the connection between smoking and heart disease. Since France was at the far end of the scale with very low heart disease mortality and

---

[*] No one would argue that the statistics imply that drunken driving should be encouraged or tolerated.

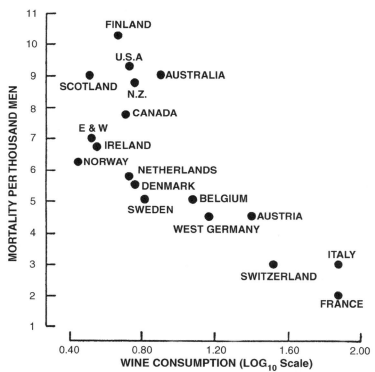

Relationship between L.H.D. mortality-rate in men aged 55–64 and wine consumption.

Reprinted from, St. Leger AS, Cochrane AL, Moore F, "Factors associated with cardiac mortality in developed countries with particular reference to the consumption of wine", The Lancet pp. 1017-1020, Copyright 1979, with permission from Elsevier.

high wine consumption, the researchers decided to re-analyze the data excluding France, on the chance that something peculiar about the French was skewing the results. But no matter how the data was filtered, nothing weakened the conclusion that *wine* reduced overall mortality and heart disease specifically, more than other forms of drinking. Stratification (a statistical analysis tool) for variables such as diet, smoking, and exercise habits did not dilute the implication that wine has some ingredient that independently protects health, or at least amplifies the alcohol effect where heart disease is concerned.

The father of the French paradox

Anti-alcohol activists were probably caught off-guard with the airing of the "French Paradox" report. Concerns over alcohol's well-known adverse social consequences and health detriments had coalesced into a mental barrier, much like the attitudes at the National Institutes of Health with the Framingham data. Following the show, wine sales and interest in wine drinking spiked dramatically. So alarmed were the policy-makers that the U.S. government reportedly contacted the French authorities and asked them to demand proof from the researcher whose work formed the basis of the story, Serge Renaud of the University of Bordeaux. Dr. Renaud was placed under considerable pressure to document his findings and his career may have been on the line had he failed. His response, published in the prestigious British medical journal *Lancet* in June 1992 confronted his critics head-on and set the foundation for a new generation of researchers. Most of what is now known about wine's health properties attributes to research inspired by Dr. Renaud's work.

In the article, Dr. Renaud summarized the data from several sources confirming that alcohol consumption lowers heart disease risk, and extended the field of view to the question of wine specifically. His own data derived from population studies around the area of Toulouse in southwestern France, where the traditional diet is high in cheese, vegetable fats, even foie gras, the extremely fatty goose or duck liver delicacy. The denizens of Toulouse nevertheless enjoy both low rates of cardiovascular issues and generous helpings of wine on a regular basis. Renaud also showed that the effects persists even in the presence of smoking, applies to both men and women, and across all age groups. Most importantly, he provided statistical evidence demonstrating that the wine drinkers of Toulouse had a more profound effect than in countries where other forms of alcohol were the primary libation. He pointed out the documented effects of alcohol on improving cholesterol profiles and blood clotting, but more significantly he opened the door to the whole issue of whether wine has some special and unique additional properties.

But southern France is not the only area with "healthy" wine-drinking patterns. Italy, parts of Spain and Greece, and other coastal Mediterranean cultures share similar dietary customs. The Mediterranean diet, known to be associated with health and longevity, includes not only regular consumption of red wine with meals but also fresh fruits, vegetables, olive oil, and fish, with generally lower levels of dairy products and red meat. Studies from these countries mirror the findings of the French populations, so it may be more accurate now to use the term "Mediterranean paradox."

The heart of the matter

Serge Renaud is not a wine researcher at heart, at least he didn't start out that way. A survey of his research publications finds a heady list of articles on heart-healthy diet factors, specifically a canola oil constituent called alpha-linolenic acid. Like many others, his initial interpretation of the seven countries study pointed to foods and habits other than wine. He tested special margarines based on alpha-linolenic acid, measuring effects on cholesterol, heart-attack risk, and even survival after heart attack. It was in fact these studies that uncovered the wine connection, leading to the famous French paradox and paving the way for a legion of wine investigators.

When I met Dr. Renaud at a wine and health conference in California's wine country, the vineyards were full of cover crops of mustard and canola, a poignant reminder that sometimes the answer is right at our feet.

One of the most prominent researchers to emerge in the field of wine and health in Dr. Renaud's footsteps is Morten Gronbaek, of the Copenhagen Heart Study and others. Although it was Renaud who provided the groundwork for the theory that red wine has special protective properties, Gronbaek set out to provide the required confirmatory data. Within a few years, Gronbaek and others published nearly two dozen papers from several countries with the same results: red wine is more protective against both heart disease and overall mortality than alcohol from other sources, but these in turn are better than abstinence in terms of cardiovascular disease and death rates. In terms of the J-curve, the bottom point—the lowest risk—is lower for wine than for beer or spirits, whose effects are comparatively weak. The studies on which this picture is based included reports from Harvard Medical School, Klatsky's Kaiser-Permanente population, and others from around the world. It should be noted that these studies were also of different types. In the next chapter we will lay out the cause-effect theory and the supportive clinical data.

Statistical variability is inevitable in every type of scientific endeavor, and so it must be acknowledged that not every study on wine and heart disease or overall mortality produced identical figures. Differences in diet, type of wine consumed, overlap between groups in terms of type of alcoholic beverage, and numerous other factors confound the findings. Sampling is inherently inconsistent to a degree also; even repeating a study using the same methods on the same population will not guarantee identical results. But remember it is the patterns, the trend that emerges when the findings are combined, that reveals the true picture.

Statisticians have a tool for doing just that, called *meta-analysis*. Basically, this method lumps together all of the relevant studies and looks at the aggregate results, thereby giving greater weight to the conclusions. Contradictory results will tend to cancel each other out this way, but if a consistent pattern appears then the conclusions are on much more solid ground. An Italian group of researchers analyzed the nineteen studies that satisfied inclusion criteria (meaning they were properly designed to eliminate bias) using meta-analysis, and concluded that overall risk of cardiovascular disease was reduced by a factor of about two-thirds compared to nondrinkers, a significant improvement over the already lower risk known to apply to alcohol drinkers in general.

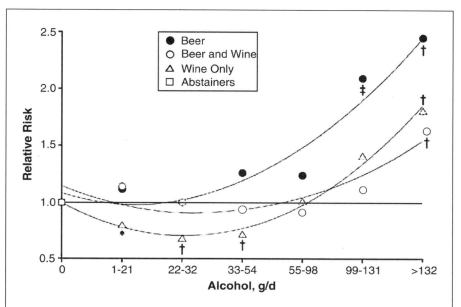

All-cause mortality risk vs. type and amount of alcohol consumption. Reproduced with permission from Renaud SC et al, *Epidemiology* 1998, ©Lippincott Williams Wilkins.

When men drink wine they are rich ... they are happy, they help their friends.

—Aristophanes

Because the focus of this early work was on cardiovascular health, many still assume that the story ends there. But that was only the beginning. Certainly, in order to live a long and productive life, a healthy heart would seem to be a requirement, and clean arteries help other organs by ensuring good blood flow. So it is worth a more detailed look at the wine/heart health connection that was the taproot of the early chapters in the wine-health story.

We have discussed how alcohol, as an independent agent, positively impacts cholesterol profiles in the right doses. With wine, the effect is amplified as compared to other alcoholic drinks. The elevation of HDL cholesterol, which helps reduce plaques in arteries, is accompanied by a correspondingly greater reduction of LDL cholesterol, the bad actor, with wine. A similar pattern is seen with the anti-clotting effect: While alcohol inhibits the aggregation of blood cells called platelets, thereby stalling the would-be clot before it starts, the effect is greater with wine. In fact, all of the major factors known to contribute to the risk of cardiovascular disease—high blood pressure, bad cholesterol, chronic inflammation, and the like—are favorably impacted by regular intake of red wine. These and other observations point to something special in wine that results in fewer heart attacks and less severe heart attacks in wine drinkers.

It is indeed the particular attributes of wine-derived compounds that legitimize the central premise of this book. But regardless of the fascinating alchemy of wine, it is more than a simple biochemical equation that shows the way to a longer and healthier life. Already I see people buying supplement pills with wine extracts, despite the fact that

Dollars and Sense

In 2006 the U.S government published the results of a study they had been doing on the cost associated with alcohol consumption for patients on Medicare (generally over age 65). They were looking to address the question of how to allocate resources in order to discourage alcohol consumption, but the results of this 5-year study suggested that they should *promote* it, especially in the form of wine. Over the five years of the study, moderate wine drinkers (those consuming 6 to 13 glasses of wine weekly) had medical costs averaging $2000 less than nondrinkers. Moderate spirits drinkers also had lower health care expenses, but at about only half of the savings realized for wine drinkers. Heavy drinkers had costs similar to those of nondrinkers. Though the researchers were surprised at the findings, this result is just another J-shaped curve! Despite the obvious implications for cost savings, Medicare has not exactly become a proponent of wine drinking.

no testing has been done to determine optimal dosing or side-effects (at least not published in the peer-reviewed literature.) We must keep in mind that this door was opened by the observation that regular, moderate wine consumption lowers the risk of disease and prolongs life, and that this lifestyle pattern is connected to a number of dietary and other factors. All of this integrates into a healthy whole, and it seems to miss the point to try to behave otherwise.

Unfortunately, the spike in red wine consumption in the U.S. following the first "French paradox" report wasn't sustained, though recent trends are encouraging. During the ensuing decade enormous progress was made in unlocking the biological mechanisms by which both alcohol and the polyphenols in red wine interact in the body. Labs around the world actively engaged the subject uncovering an array of additional unexpected findings in areas as diverse as cancer, diabetes, and even influenza and other infectious diseases. The ways in which wine slows down the mental deterioration of aging, even the aging process itself, are being threshed out, and the possibilities seem to expand with each new finding.

If a man refrains from wine to such an extent that he does serious harm to his nature, he will not be free from blame.
—Saint Thomas Aquinas

Chapter 5

The Phenomenal Phenolics

No thing more excellent or valuable than wine was ever granted mankind by God.

—Plato

We can say with some confidence now that wine has unique characteristics that impart health benefits beyond those attributable to other alcoholic (and non-alcoholic) beverages. In this chapter, our purpose is to establish the plausible cause-and-effect explanation. Simply identifying an association isn't enough to guide us without knowing the "how" and "why" of the relationship. It will be helpful to add to our understanding of the long-recognized cardiovascular health observations, but research in recent years has taken the field into unexpected areas. Why is wine so uniquely helpful against conditions as diverse as osteoporosis, peptic ulcers, and cancer?

Wine polyphenols are known to be potent antioxidants, which may help to explain why wine is special, but this aspect too only sets the stage for more intriguing and surprising recent discoveries. Neither alcohol nor antioxidant activity adequately explain wine's full range of properties alone. There must be something else going on, and polyphenols—an extended family of related molecules that make wine what it is—are the prime candidate for our hypothesis that something unique in wine explains the epidemiologic data. Despite the chemical-sounding name, polyphenols (also called phenolics) are found in a variety of foods, and they play a central role in a new understanding of nutrition and aging.

What are phenolics?

Red wine is an almost unfathomably complex elixir. How else could there be so many different flavor profiles, so many nuances from only a handful of grape varieties? Practiced oenophiles can identify the place of origin, vintage year, even the signature of the vintner from the smell (bouquet) and taste of the wine. There are probably thousands of different substances in a typical wine, and they change as the wine evolves with aging. When nature conspires with the art and science of the winemaker, the result is a concoction of biochemicals that defies cold scientific analysis. Expert winemakers will be the first to admit that they do not *make* wine so much as they help guide a natural and still partly mysterious process.

A great many of the substances in wine have been characterized, however. Many of them are in a class of organic molecules labeled "aromatic," which has specific meaning in chemistry as well as describing one of the properties they contribute to wine. Aromatic molecules typically have at least one ring of carbon atoms, which tends to make them somewhat volatile; this gives rise to the "nose" or bouquet of the wine. (Some large wine glasses are specifically designed to optimally capture the nose of specific types of wine.) The aromatic properties are reflected in the names of some of these compounds, such as vanillic acid, rosemarinic acid, and cinnamates. Ever heard of a wine described as having a "floral" nose? Perhaps it contained the polyphenols *geraniin* or *petunidin*.

When wine critics use such colorful prose to describe wine characteristics, they don't actually stretch the truth as much as one might assume. The polyphenols that constitute a wine's flavor and color profile are in fact the same ones that exist in other botanical sources. Wines with a cherry-like note have the same polyphenols as cherries do, and so forth. What is so remarkable is how many of them can be expressed in the *Vitis vinifera* grape.

Wine is one of the most civilized things in the world and one of the natural things of the world that has been brought to the greatest perfection, and it offers a greater range for enjoyment and appreciation than, possibly, any other purely sensory thing.
— Ernest Hemingway, *Death in the Afternoon*

Flower power

An important subset of the polyphenol family is the group of compounds that give color to flowers and plants. For example, *delphinidin* is the phenolic that gives delphiniums their characteristic blue color. Blueberries are an excellent source of dietary polyphenols, and all red berried fruit is pigmented by phenolics, as are many other fruits and vegetables.

The building block for these molecules is a specific six-sided carbon ring structure (benzene ring) and the version representing the simplest basic unit is *phenol*. When there is more than one of these hexagonal units in the structure, it is known as a *polyphenol**. There is an enormous variety of these plant-derived substances. One of the better-known categories is the *flavonoids*, which have a specific three-ring base structure. (Recall that citrus-derived flavonoids were found to aid in reversal of scurvy from vitamin C deficiency.) *Tannins*, which give the "pucker" to wine and tea, are actually defined by their ability to combine with proteins in animal skin to make leather, and are generally within the polyphenol family. Wine critics go to great lengths to describe the contributions of tannins to a wine's flavor profile. Green and white tea are known to be excellent sources of anti-oxidant tannins, and consequently much research has been directed at the role of tea in disease prevention.

Each of these categories encompasses a long list of variants and combinations. Many of the individual substances have been isolated and studied intensively, but it is not completely known to what degree

---

*   The terms *polyphenol* and *phenolic* are not strictly the same but are used interchangeably here for convenience. Likewise, *flavonols* are a subset of *flavonoids*, but the distinction is not critical to our purposes.

the biological actions occur in isolation and what the interactions and synergies of them are in their natural milieu. It is important to keep this in mind as we review the studies on polyphenols and health. Much remains to be learned on this subject, but what is already known is exciting if not yet widely appreciated.

Because many of the polyphenols are pigments, they impart color to wine, which is of course why red wine is preferred as a dietary source; white wine has comparatively low levels. Others, as mentioned, are more associated with aroma, while tannins give what is known as "mouth feel" or texture to the wine. All of these contribute to the characteristic astringency and brighter color of youthful red wine, and over time they evolve into more subdued forms. A common question is whether different red wines have greater or lesser amounts of beneficial phenolics, but it appears that overall, the location of the vineyard and the techniques

WINE POLYPHENOLS

Flavonoids

Quercetin

Catechins

Anthocyanins

Procyanidins

Non-Flavonoids

Cinnamates

Caffeic acid

Genistic acid

Vanillic acid

Tannins

Trihydroxystilbenes

Resveratrol

Polydatin

of viticulture—contributors to what is called *terroir*, or the distinctive sense of place—seem to have a greater impact than the varietal. So in general it doesn't matter so much whether you are drinking a pinot noir or a cabernet sauvignon, as long as it is red.

A fair question is why red wine is associated with high levels of polyphenols compared to, say, unfermented grape juice. There are several reasons for this: Firstly, the grapes that are grown for juice (similar to table grapes) are generally varieties that are selected for fruitiness and sweetness with a minimum of the bitter flavors contributed by many polyphenols. These same substances are actually preferred in wine grapes (*vinifera* species) as they add complexity and depth to the wine.

As we will see, polyphenols are part of the natural defenses of the grape against fungal infections and other environmental insults, and *vinifera* vines are sometimes intentionally "stressed" in order to encourage the development of polyphenols. Vines may be planted in rocky soil, for example. Or vineyard managers might "drop" fruit, that is they prune off a percentage of the grape clusters when they are immature so the vine will focus its efforts on the remaining bunches, resulting in greater concentration of polyphenols (and hence, flavor.) Table grapes, on the other hand, are often more pampered and sprayed to keep the stress level, and thereby the polyphenol content down, and crop yields high.

So wine grapes have a higher polyphenol content to begin with. These are concentrated in the skins, where they serve their function as guardians against diseases, and in the seeds (ostensibly so that they can survive long enough to sprout in the Spring while their fruit envelope perishes.) Winemakers sometimes pay special attention to the crushing technique with regard to the seeds, which impart a more bitter character from their polyphenols. For white wine, the juice is typically separated from the skins and seeds before fermentation. Rosé wines experience a brief contact for just a bit of color and body. To make red wine, however, the "must" is fermented in contact with the skins, a process known as maceration (or "extraction"). This is one area where the winemaker exerts some influence, deciding for example how often to "punch down" the

The Ripe Stuff

The question of when to harvest wine grapes has gotten a lot more complicated in recent years. Traditionally, sugar levels were the primary indicator, with the precise timing related to weather and logistical considerations. With any fruit, when it is sweet enough it is usually ripe enough, flavorful and juicy. But the polyphenols that give the eventual wine its flavors and texture may develop at a different rate than sugars, often more slowly; this additional consideration, based on polyphenol content, is known as "phenolic ripeness." All of the things that wine growers do to stress the vines and encourage the development of polyphenols affect phenolic ripeness, and getting the timing to align with sugar levels (physiologic ripeness) is a balancing act. In the traditional winegrowing regions of Europe, grape varieties and local growing conditions have the comfort of a long marriage, so harvest based on sugar levels usually works. But hot weather, for example, can push sugar levels up quickly, while phenolics take longer to fully develop, or a cooler than usual season may have the opposite effect.

What makes it more difficult is that wine drinkers, and the wine critics who often determine the commercial success of a wine, are increasingly looking for more concentrated and intense flavors. Often this means that growers delay picking past the point of physiologic ripeness, thereby giving the grapes more "hang time" in order to concentrate the phenolics. But the higher sugar levels that result translate into higher alcohol levels with fermentation. Traditional wines may have had an alcohol content of around 12-13%, but it is now not unusual to see wines with more than 16%. Some winemakers actually put the wine through a process called reverse osmosis, sort of like dialysis, to reduce alcohol levels. From a health point of view, the higher polyphenol content is a good thing, but the additional alcohol, not so much.

skins as they float to the top of the vat, or how long the maceration period will be before the juice is filtered off. It is this extended contact with the seeds and skins that elevates the polyphenol content even higher.

Alcohol serves an important role in polyphenol development in the nascent wine also. As the sugars ferment, the rising alcohol level acts as a solvent to further extract the emerging polyphenols into the solution. And the fermentation process itself is required for the formation of certain phenolics which are not present in meaningful quantities in the virgin grape. Aging in oak barrels may contribute to enhancing the polyphenol content as well.

Skin deep

Grapes are subject to a variety of challenges during their growth. A number of pathogens such as *phylloxera* mites attack the vine itself (in this case the roots), but the flesh of the grape is an inviting target for many types of bacteria, viruses, and fungi. Ultraviolet radiation from too much direct sun exposure can also be damaging, and flavonoids have a special ability to block the most harmful portion of the UV spectrum. So the adaptive response of the plant is to concentrate anti-oxidant polyphenols in the skin of the fruit. Many of these same anti-oxidant polyphenols are now available in skin care products for human skin, which is of course subject to many of the same environmental stresses. There is evidence to support the claim that wine polyphenols are quite effective in this application, and this is another area of active research.

A report in *Lancet* in 1993 first drew attention to the superiority of wine polyphenols as antioxidants. Many still assume that the best anti-oxidants available are vitamins. But wine polyphenols have been tested against antioxidant vitamins in several "head-to-head" studies and are consistently found to be many times more potent. One good example is a study from Scotland published in the *American Journal of Clinical Nutrition* in 1998. This group developed a model using human white blood cells in a tissue culture, with the cells subjected to a standardized oxidative insult that resulted in predictable and measurable damage to the cells' DNA. They then added either vitamin C or various polyphenols determine whether there was any protective effect when the cells were exposed to the oxidizing chemical. All of the polyphenols tested were significantly more effective at reducing oxidative DNA damage, some up to 9 times greater than vitamin C.

Other studies comparing wine polyphenols to the anti-oxidant vitamins A and E have found these vitamins to be much less potent also. In fact, *no dietary anti-oxidants have yet been identified that are more effective than wine polyphenols.* For this reason, wine polyphenols are commonly referred to as "wine anti-oxidants." But as I have indicated, the oxidative theory of aging and disease is likely only part of the picture. Rather than this being a point of departure for the polyphenol contribution, though, this story is only beginning. Reducing oxidative damage through dietary means and skin care certainly makes sense, but new research indicates that polyphenols have a range of fascinating capabilities that are only now beginning to be characterized.

Antioxidant properties of wine polyphenols are likely responsible for a range of other effects of interest to plastic surgeons and their patients too. A group from Ohio State University provided evidence in a 2002 report that procyanidin phenolics in particular enhanced wound healing through their ability to modulate oxidation. Another report, published in 2003, found that another polyphenol may be helpful in the treatment and prevention of abnormal scars called keloids. A condition called radiation fibrosis, a sort of scarring that is a sequela of radiation therapy for cancer, may also respond to polyphenol power. This is a significant and potentially very useful finding, as thousands of cancer patients suffer from radiation fibrosis, which can be painful and sometimes debilitating. (Wine polyphenols have some impressive anti-cancer effects as well, discussed in chapter 7.)

Other properties of polyphenols that likely relate to their antioxidant capacities include protection of the kidneys (according to researchers from Italy and the University of Connecticut), improvement in lung function (especially in chronic inflammatory conditions), and lowered cataract risk—by about half—according to a 2005 study from Iceland. No doubt numerous other benefits remain to be identified.

The questions that polyphenol researchers are addressing now are less directed at whether these compounds are superior anti-oxidants or why, but how they work in other unique and interesting ways. For example, one clinical trial reported in 2003 used a polyphenol-rich grape seed extract supplement on patients with high cholesterol. All subjects experienced significant reductions in their levels of oxidized LDL cholesterol, as we would expect based upon the earlier studies. These same researchers then went on to identify a gene associated with atherosclerosis and activated by oxidized LDL. The grape seed extract was also found to inhibit expression of the gene. The implication is that the properties of polyphenols are not entirely attributable to direct interactions with "bad" molecules such as free radicals or cholesterol, but are working at the more fundamental level of DNA transcription. Other studies have also suggested that modulation of genetic expression (called "signal transduction" by biochemists) is a significant function of wine polyphenols, for a variety of processes in addition to those related to vascular disease. Wine phenolics are actually directing the switching on and of genes in our genetic code! This may turn out to be far more important in the long run.

As previously mentioned, antioxidants do help curtail the growth of atherosclerotic plaques, because oxidized LDL cholesterol and free radical activity within the lesion are known abettors. But the persuasive influence of polyphenol antioxidants is by itself an insufficient deterrent. Part of the formative reaction is driven by another chemical messenger system called *endothelins*. These inflammatory provocateurs also appear to be thwarted by polyphenols extracted from either red wine or cocoa, according to a 2001 study from London, and others. Minus encouragement by endothelins, cholesterol plaque formation is discouraged.

We know from the epidemiological patterns that not only does wine, with its polyphenols, lower the odds of a cardiac event, but it improves the odds of surviving one when it does occur. This requires a separate explanation. As with the multi-pronged attack against atherosclerosis, it is likely that several modes of action are at work, but among the most interesting is one which brings us back to the anti-aging front: heat shock proteins. (Recall that these proteins are responsible for a number of remarkable anti-aging effects.) When a coronary artery is occluded and the heart muscle is deprived of oxygen-containing blood, damage begins to set in which culminates in death or permanent injury of the muscle cells. Recovery depends upon how long the period of oxygen starvation lasts. Heat shock proteins, which are induced by wine polyphenols, effectively extend this period, allowing for better recovery of muscle function.

One group of researchers at the University of Sienna in Italy discovered another possibly significant effect of polyphenols on heart muscle. They looked for ways in which the tissue might be pre-conditioned to better survive an oxygen deficiency episode. What they found was that polyphenols did exactly that, by stimulating the formation of a molecule called *adenosine.* This is a naturally occurring compound, actually used as a drug in cardiac resuscitation. Wine phenolics encourage the body to make more of its own. Adenosine is a short-lived molecule, however so the linkage to regular wine consumption may be particularly important if this effect is to be meaningful.

When blood flow is restored, though, the event isn't over. The toxins that accumulate in the tissue during oxygen deprivation spill out and do further damage, much of it probably mediated by free radicals. This is known as "ischemia-reperfusion" injury.* Polyphenols have been found to be remarkably effective at limiting this phenomenon, providing another plausible contribution to the improved muscle survival and function. Interestingly, this makes a connection to plastic surgery, because the sometimes elaborate rearrangement of tissues required for reconstructive procedures often requires that the repositioned parts undergo periods of ischemia and reperfusion. (I am unaware, however, of anyone employing polyphenols for this purpose, though there is good evidence of their effectiveness. I do not recommend that my patients drink wine before surgery, due to the potential for interference with blood clotting.)

---

* Ischemia, pronounced "iss-**kee**-mee-a, is the term for lack of oxygen from absent or inadequate blood flow; reperfusion is restoration of blood flow.

Unfortunately, many people simply don't like red wine. There are many potential reasons—including the possibility that they haven't ever been exposed to *good* red wine—but one frequently cited reason is the characteristic astringent sensation associated with "tannic" wines. For connoisseurs, this is perceived as giving "structure" to the wine, something to balance out the fruity flavor components, while for others it is less appealing. The sensation is largely the result of a phenomenon called *protein binding*. Certain wine polyphenols have an affinity for attaching themselves to protein molecules, a natural embrace encouraged by their 3-dimensional configuration. Saliva contains abundant quantities of a digestive enzyme protein called amylase, which is readily bound up by wine phenolics, which in turn causes the dry sensation on the tongue and cheeks. Another protein molecule to which polyphenols eagerly attach is LDL cholesterol.[*] This is a separate and additional effect from the antioxidant activity which is known to reduce levels of oxidized LDL. Protein-polyphenol complexation may also help to explain the specific anti-Alzheimer's disease effect (chapter 8), by targeting a protein called beta-amyloid which attacks brain cells.

Cranberry juice is another drink with a characteristic astringent "mouth feel," to borrow a phrase from the wine tasting vernacular. Cranberry juice has its own array of healthful properties, including the long-held notion that it can prevent urinary tract infections. There is in fact some good evidence to support this belief, but not in the way that is often assumed. Because cranberry juice (like wine) is acidic, the theory was that it acidified the urine, suppressing bacterial growth. Evidence now points to the protein binding effect of cranberry-derived polyphenols, as they attach themselves to proteins on bacteria thereby neutralizing them. It seems doubtful that this could replace antibiotic therapy but as a preventive health measure it does make some sense. By inference, then, red wine with its higher polyphenol content should also

---

[*] Recall that LDL stands for Low-Density lipo*protein*, so cholesterol particles are actually protein-fat complexes; the protein is the carriage and the cholesterol particle is the passenger.

be an effective aid for a healthy bladder, though direct evidence for this has not yet been presented.*

Other bacteria are known to be suppressed by polyphenols, presumably by protein binding. For example, a strain known as *Strep. mutans* is associated with dental decay, because the formation of plaque on the teeth is facilitated by an enzyme that the Strep bacterium secretes. Wine polyphenols have a high affinity for binding and thereby inhibiting the activity of this enzyme, so purple teeth may actually be a good thing, as least as far as prevention of cavities is concerned.**

A little farther down the line we find perhaps an even greater surprise. Standard medical advice for patients with peptic ulcers has traditionally included things such as avoidance of spicy foods and, of course, alcoholic beverages. However, a few years ago our understanding of the causes of ulcer disease was realigned by the discovery that a bacterium called *Helicobacter pylori* was associated with the majority of ulcers. Previously, the assumption was that ulcers were more purely related to over-secretion of digestive acids, hence the guidance to avoid alcohol and other gastric stimulants. Some wine polyphenols turn out to be potent inhibitors of *Helicobacter,* and, as in the case of *Strep mutans,* the toxin that it manufactures. So perhaps the notion of an *aperitif* before eating or *digestif* after a meal is scientifically defensible, as long as it is wine-based.

Viruses have a different *modus operandi* than bacteria. Because they are actually inert particles and not living organisms, in order for them to

---

*   For this effect to work, the polyphenols would have to be excreted intact into the urine. Recent work finds that cranberry juice neither acidifies the urine nor contains measurable polyphenol anti-bacterial activity, despite clinical evidence of effectiveness. More remains to be understood about the effect of polyphenols in suppressing urinary tract infections.

**   Although there is good published evidence of wine polyphenol activity against *Strep mutans*, not all studies are in concurrence. A June 2007 report from the University of Pavia in Italy suggested that acids present in both red and white wine are the active antibacterial agents. Either way, wine was good for dental health.

replicate and conduct their business, they have to commandeer a living cell's metabolic and reproductive machinery and turn it to their own purposes. This requires an act of biologic burglary: that is, they have to somehow penetrate the cell's membrane and get inside. They accomplish this act of hijacking by binding certain proteins on the cell's surface that function as "sentries" for points of entry. Once in, millions more viruses are churned out by the hapless victim cell.

This process introduces another potentially important arena for polyphenol activity, as it has been shown that some polyphenols have an ability to bind viral proteins, thereby rendering them impotent. Cell surface proteins are targeted also, blocking the access points for viral penetration. This phenomenon has been observed in laboratory studies with a variety of viruses including HIV (Human Immunodeficiency Virus), Herpes Simplex, and others. The effectiveness of polyphenol antiviral activity in living systems remains to be proven, however, and it is common for laboratory findings (*in vitro*) to fall flat when applied clinically (*in vivo*). So it would be foolhardy to conclude that any potential protection afforded by red wine equates to safe sex (even if it may facilitate the opportunity for it.)

Cold Hard Facts

Wine drinkers also have a lower incidence of the common cold (caused by a "rhinoviruses") according to a 2002 study from Spain. This was a cohort study involving more than 4,000 faculty and staff at 5 Spanish universities. Consumers of more than 2 glasses of wine a day were only about half as likely to suffer a cold as teetotalers, and the correlation was stronger for red wine than for white. No relationship to other alcoholic drinks was identified, and confounding variables were accounted for, so a special role for red wine is imputed. Laboratory studies have shown anti-rhinoviral activity of wine flavonoids, so again the epidemiologic inference finds a plausible cause-effect explanation. (Contrast this to the common wisdom of using vitamin C as an anti-cold remedy, which as we have noted lacks both clinical evidence of efficacy and a laboratory-confirmed model of how it might work.)

Start your enzymes

Since all metabolic processes are modulated by enzymes, the proteins that facilitate chemical reactions in living organisms such as people, polyphenol-protein binding may have profound and as yet undiscovered influence on a number of critical metabolic systems. Some are well-known, an example of this being found in the COX enzyme system, inhibited to a degree by alcohol (as we have observed) but more so by certain polyphenols. An easily observed result of this is moderation of blood clotting. More importantly, these enzymes are centrally involved in chronic inflammatory reactions, via a hormone system called *prostaglandins*. It is a process that is upstream of a long cascade of metabolic events of importance. These inflammatory reactions are implicated in the underlying causes of many of the degenerative disorders, such as the growth of plaques in the coronary arteries that

---

Biologic Properties of Polyphenols

Antibacterial

Neutralize bacterial toxins

Anti-fungal

Antiviral

Modulate wound healing

Antioxidant

Anti-cancer

Regulation of gene expression (signal transduction)

Hormone effects (phytoestrogen)

Anti-aging (sirtuin activation)

Endothelin inactivation (vascular health)

Anticoagulant

Ischemia-reperfusion

Up-regulation of heat shock proteins

---

end up triggering the clots in the first place. So inhibition of clotting is useful, but more so the prevention of the stimulus to the clot. With wine we get both.

Because of the ability of polyphenols to route prostaglandin production in a more favorable direction by virtue of their actions on COX enzymes, their antioxidant capacity will likely be recognized as a less significant function despite the intensity of that effect. In this case, antioxidants are working downstream. Epidemiologic data suggests that wine has unique capabilities beyond those that can be satisfyingly explained by alcohol and polyphenol antioxidant activity. It is important that we explore these features in some detail if we are to continue to make the case that red wine is central to an anti-aging strategy, because there are of course other options to consider for antioxidant therapies, even if they are less effective and arguably less appealing, and more efficient means of alcohol ingestion than lingering over a meal with a glass or two of pinot.

A flavonoid with flair

As the best studied of the flavonoid polyphenols, *quercetin* is the flagship phenolic of the category. Although it is believed to be a less effective antioxidant, quercetin may have some unique capabilities. Quercetin and other flavonoids, the co-factors along with vitamin C in reversal of scurvy, occur in substantial amounts in many red wines. There are fewer studies on quercetin specifically (resveratrol having hogged the limelight), but flavonoids have been the subject of some attention for years, and are more familiar to many.

The discussions in the early to mid-twentieth century (when the identity and specific properties of vitamins were being discovered) as to whether flavonoids should be considered a vitamin may be worth reviving. All that was truly known at that time was that there existed a class of flavonoid compounds, with unique properties; the identities of the key players such as quercetin had not yet been elucidated. But imagine the controversy that might erupt over placing "recommended daily allowance" vitamin content on wine labels! As more information comes forth about the range of health properties of all wine polyphenols, a vigorous debate along these lines is in fact in progress.*

It is hard to not be impressed when cataloguing the ever-expanding list of scientifically documented health and anti-aging capabilities of wine phenolics. We can comfortably claim that the criterion of a plausible cause-effect explanation for the epidemiologic associations of lowered disease risk and longer life span with wine has been amply demonstrated. Laboratory studies from around the world provide confirmatory evidence. We can promote our hypothesis to "theory" status, in scientific terms a proven explanation that in this case points the way to clinical testing and practical applications.

What we need to remember is that not everything observed in a test tube or a laboratory animal works the same way in the human, and that there are numerous other variables especially in view of the complexities of human behavior. Not everyone who drinks red wine regularly will live to be 100, wine will not prevent the flu or heart attack in everybody, and sometimes people with all of the right lifestyle choices get sick anyway. The anecdotal form of evidence is meaningless for these reasons; there will always be exceptions. But if our goal is improved quality of life along with long life, the odds are definitely in favor of wine drinkers and for good reason.

> *Wine is the living blood of the grape. Wine is harmony; a marvelously complex and well-balanced blend of ever so many different substances in a solution of water and alcohol.*
> —Andre Simon (The Art of Good Living, 1924)

---

* In the U.S., wine bottle labels must be approved by the Department of Treasury's Alcohol and Tobacco Tax and Trade Bureau (formerly the Bureau of Alcohol, Tobacco and Firearms,). The ATF has long been opposed to any label content referring to potential health properties of wine, even listing resveratrol content, the mere mention of which might be construed as relating somehow to health.

Chapter 6

Resveratrol Revelations:
How a Particularly Potent Polyphenol
Rocked the Scientific World

I wonder often what the vintners buy one half so precious as the goods they sell.

—Omar Khayyyam, *The Rubiyat*

Only a handful of the myriad substances in wine have been studied extensively in isolation. One of the more interesting is the polyphenol resveratrol, which has received so much press as an anti-aging agent that it is practically a household word among those "of a certain age." Resveratrol occurs in fairly high concentrations in rich red wines, and is present also in liverworts and many other higher plant species including peanuts. However, with the exception of wine grapes and a few others, resveratrol is usually concentrated in the non-edible parts of the plant. A wide array of pharmacologic properties has been identified with resveratrol, and it is likely the basis for various herbal folk remedies and traditional Chinese apothecary medicines used for centuries.

Resveratrol made headlines in 2001 with the first reports of its effectiveness against cancer cells (Chapter 8). Hundreds of research papers on resveratrol have been published since then, at last count totaling more than 1600 articles in the medical literature. Even more exciting than the anti-cancer properties are the more recent findings about the biological mechanisms of lifespan extension, which is central to the theme of this book: Recall that for decades, scientists have known that *caloric restriction* significantly prolongs lifespan in experimental animals (Chapter 2). In other words, if one takes for example a laboratory rat (whose physiology is closer to humans in many more ways than we like to think) and restrict its diet by 30-40% lower total calorie intake, it will outlive rats fed *ad libitum* by a similar percentage. (For humans, this would extrapolate to a potential lifespan of 130 years and beyond.) The phenomenon applies to all types of animals studied to date, suggesting that something of fundamental biological importance is at work.

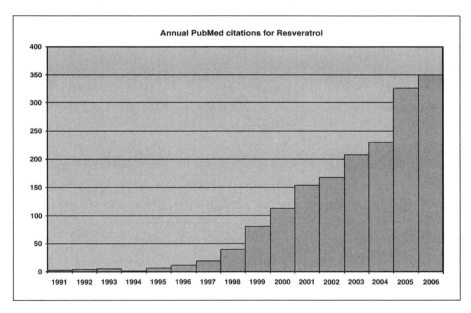

Scientists now believe they know how this occurs. A system of enzymes, called *sirtuins*, is activated by this drastic reduction of food intake. Molecular biologist Leonard Guarente of the Massachusetts Institute of Technology (MIT) discovered the sirtuin gene, called *Sir1*, in 1995. It took a bit more detective work to figure out exactly how these enzymes work; they appear to be involved in regulation of genes that control energy and metabolism, and a cascade of events that trigger the longevity effect through a sort of survival adaptation to periods of inadequate food supply, such as with famine or drought. The whole notion that a small number of genes could have profound effects on longevity was inspired by the earlier reports that manipulating a single gene doubled the lifespan of a type of worm (Chapter 2). It began to appear that aging might not be such an intractably complex problem after all, and the prospect of gene manipulation to advantageous effect suddenly seemed less far-fetched.

So the "holy grail" for anti-aging researchers became a quest to find ways of activating the sirtuin system without the inconvenience of semi-starvation. The fact that sirtuins are of such basic import is of benefit in studying the functions of these enzymes, since they are virtually identical in everything from bacteria to humans.[*] Scientists call this phenomenon "evolutionary conservation" meaning that as more complex organisms develop, the most important systems remain essentially unchanged. A useful model to start out with for the role of sirtuins on longevity is brewer's yeast, whose lifespan is measured in days so that one doesn't have to wait months or years to see the effects of anything that might impact it.

A group at Harvard Medical School set out to do just that. It was one of Dr. Guarente's research fellows, David Sinclair, who took up the challenge. After refining the experimental model with yeast cultures (*Saccharomyces cervisiae*, or brewer's yeast) Sinclair's group systematically exposed the cultures to various biochemicals. After an exhaustive analysis involving thousands of chemical candidates, resveratrol emerged as the best trigger for the sirtuins, resulting in prolongation of the life cycle of the yeast organisms. The only other activators with any effect at all were other wine polyphenols. The report was published in the major medical journal *Nature* in 2003 and widely celebrated. Their work was followed up with studies in a more complex lifeform (and another favorite of researchers), a worm known as *C. elegans*. (Yes, whoever named this species thought that a worm could be described as "elegant.") Again the lifespan was extended, along with sirtuin activation by resveratrol. Fruit flies were up

---

[*] There are in fact several distinct sirtuins and they have varied functions in higher and lower organisms, but categorically they fulfill analogous roles and are molecularly similar.

next, with the same result, followed by a certain type of fish; this latter being an important step, since vertebrates are more complex creatures.

The next step is to see whether this applies at all in animals such as mammals (e.g., humans). These types of studies of course take longer to do, since the natural lifespan is measured in years rather than days or weeks. Progress in this investigation was reported in late 2006 from Sinclair's group, again in *Nature*. This particular study examined the question of not only can the effect be replicated in laboratory mice, but whether it could apply in the face of a high-calorie, high-fat diet. Resveratrol measurably shifted the physiology of mice on the unhealthy diet to more closely match those on a standard diet. The only catch was the fact that very high doses—equivalent to 100 bottles of red wine a day—were required.

It remains to be shown, of course, whether this will work in humans and whether high doses are safe. Of central importance with the resveratrol-sirtuin mechanism for any living thing is the concept of dose-response, since as one would expect different doses produce varying results. Polyphenols, like any nutrient or drug, must be toxic at some level. This mirrors the J-shaped curve with alcohol in humans, beneficial up to a point and detrimental with escalating doses beyond that. Much remains to be determined before artificially high intake of a polyphenol can be recommended, but following the news of the resveratrol mouse study, supplements flew off health-food store shelves, and announcements of new formulations appear on the newswires almost daily.

It appeared to most, then, that the whole question had been wrapped up in a nice neat package, and we only need wait a bit longer for conclusive evidence that resveratrol is indeed the Methuselah molecule. Sirtuins regulate lifespan, resveratrol activates sirtuins, organisms fed resveratrol live longer, problem solved, Nobel Prize committee taking notice. But with science things are rarely so tidy, and a cautionary note has been sounded by two of Guarente's other protégés, Matt Kaeberlein and Brian Kennedy, both now at the University of Washington in Seattle. While at Guarente's lab, Kaeberlein and Kennedy published a paper suggesting that the resveratrol effect on yeast cultures was not in fact related to sirtuins at all. They contend that the result is an artifact of the testing method. It's a bit tricky to explain, but basically it works like this: In order to determine if a certain protein (for instance, a sirtuin enzyme) is active, a molecule is attached to it that glows (fluoresces) when it is doing its thing. Resveratrol may cause this fluorescence in the absence of the sirtuins however, giving what scientists call a false-positive result.

Manipulating sirtuins holds fascinating prospects though, and Guarente cofounded a company called *Elixir* in 1999 in order to try to bring the idea to commercial fruition. Sinclair, meanwhile, was plunging forward with his resveratrol romance, claiming that someday we would all be taking resveratrol like miracle vitamins. He does bring some credibility to his view, in that while working with Guarente he helped determine the precise mechanism of action of one of the sirtuins, *Sir2*. This particular enzyme counters the accumulation of broken DNA fragments, which build up in organisms as they age and disrupt things to the point of eventual fatality. Others in the lab found different important capabilities for *Sir2*, connecting sirtuins more directly to energy metabolism.

Sinclair went on to start his own company, Sirtris Pharmaceuticals, banking on the resveratrol-sirtuin connection. Others have banked on the idea too, to the tune of $103 million in venture capital financing and an initial public stock offering for another $62 million. Their stated goal isn't to make life-extending products, which would be impossible to prove in humans anyway, but rather to prove that pharmaceutical-grade products derived from resveratrol can prevent certain degenerative diseases. The widely circulated report that the mice on a high-fat diet could be made healthy with massive doses seemed to bolster their case.

But what of the mice on a normal diet? Did resveratrol extend their lifespan? This data was not included in the report, which was based on findings one year into the study; since mice normally life 2-3 years, those numbers came later. As of this writing, they have not been published but have been disclosed at scientific meetings, and the word on the street is that there was no effect even at substantial doses.

This comes as no surprise to Matt Kaeberlien, who nevertheless acknowledges that resveratrol is a remarkable molecule with fascinating possibilities. When I asked him what he made of Sinclair's report, he offered a possible alternative explanation: the high-fat diet given the mice was more than unhealthy, it may have been so noxious as to cause inflammation of the liver and other organs; resveratrol was able to reverse these toxic effects, perhaps through its remarkable antioxidant capabilities, but in ways unrelated to sirtuin activation. And he points out that others have not been able to reproduce the longevity effect of resveratrol in yeast and other organisms, but negative results tend not to be published. Perhaps the idea of the resveratrol-sirtuin effect is so appealing that no one wants to rain on the parade.

Confused yet? Join the club. Clearly, a lot remains to be done in order to sort all this out. Guarente, meanwhile, has joined forces with Sinclair at Sirtris, so they must be on to something. The pharmaceutical giant GlaxoSmithKline thought so too, and bought the company for more than $700 million in 2008. Sirtris is developing a number of synthetic molecules very similar to resveratrol in an attempt to boost the effectiveness, and some intriguing early reports have been published. A study published in November 2008 found that one of these derivatives protected mice on high-fat diets from becoming obese, while enhancing their exercise tolerance, just as resveratrol does but in lower doses. They attributed this to activated sirtuins enhancing the stability of DNA by repairing accumulated breaks related to aging, while simultaneously keeping it neatly packed and organized. Clinical trials have already been initiated for some of these compounds.

But there is a lot more to the resveratrol story than the prospect of miraculous lifespan extension or protection from obesity. The potential to counter the effects of a toxic diet on the liver is certainly nothing to sniff at. One study has been published showing that resveratrol might even help reverse the effects of the poison dioxin (believed to be the agent used in the attempted assassination of Ukranian President Yushenko in 2004). Nevertheless, it is fairly certain that the resveratrol that Sirtris brings to market with the FDA's approval will not be the same as what you can buy on the internet or at health food stores. For now, then, we return to the source—the grapes and the bottle.

In wine grapes, resveratrol is produced in response to stress from bacterial attack or fungal colonization, most likely due to its ability to combat infection. In other words, like penicillin, resveratrol is a natural antibiotic. More recent studies on polyphenol antiviral activity, and specifically resveratrol, have uncovered additional mechanisms of action. We have good evidence that antioxidant actions and protein binding both work against viruses, but a 2005 study from Italy published in *The Journal of Infectious Diseases* evaluated effects against influenza viruses *in vitro* as well as *in vivo* tests in mice. They discovered that resveratrol worked within the infected cell to disrupt the process of viral DNA transcription, a necessary step for viral replication. Mice inoculated with the flu virus and then given resveratrol fared much better than their control group counterparts. In fact, about half of the untreated mice succumbed to the virus, while there were no deaths in the resveratrol-treated cohort. If the same hold true in the human model, then perhaps the standard advice to drinks lots of liquids should specify that some be in the form of red wine, or at least the traditional chicken soup prescription could be upgraded to a *coq a vin*.

Resveratrol and diabetes

Chances are you know someone who is diabetic. Type 1 ("juvenile") diabetes, the type that has its onset in youth and requires daily shots of insulin, has remained a persistent problem, while type 2–the type related to adult obesity–has increased in prevalence along with Americans' expanding waistlines. Fortunately for many of us, wine drinkers tend to maintain a healthy weight, but wine may turn out to have a therapeutic role as well. Much of this relates to specific properties of resveratrol, but there are some other things to consider first.

Food, primarily carbohydrates, is processed into a sugar known as glucose, which in turn fuels the body. Insulin is required in order to move the glucose from the blood stream into the cells where it is metabolically "burned" thereby releasing energy. In type 1, the body doesn't make enough insulin, and in type 2, there is resistance to its effects. Foods that rapidly raise blood sugar are especially problematic. Although alcohol is a carbohydrate, it has its own unique metabolic pathway that minimizes impact on blood sugar levels. One might even make the case that alcohol is a preferred dietary fuel.

A predilection for prediction

A familiar story to the reader by this point is the discovery that new revelations have almost always been anticipated by someone with exceptional foresight and a penchant for defying conventional wisdom. One such individual was Salvatore Lucia, a professor of medicine at the University of California who published a book in 1954 called *Wine as Food and Medicine* (The Blakiston Company, New York and Toronto). It is a remarkably comprehensive view and expounds in detail about alcohol, wine and diabetes. He points out the useful notion that alcohol has lower calories per unit weight than carbohydrates, and is metabolized differently.

Dr. Lucia also anticipated the chemical revolution that would reveal why wine occupies such a special place in diet, health and life; he wrote "Perhaps there is a relationship between the structure of some of the chemical compounds found in so kaleidoscopic a mixture as wine" and the myriad reactions to it. He also placed the role of wine in an appropriate context: "In the wild scramble for therapeutic specificity, little thought has been given to psychotherapeutic effects of the simple adjuvants to living that make life worth while." He bemoaned the "frenetic mode of living" (long before freeways, fast food, and cell phones) and observed that "partaking of wine offers an opportunity for psychic rest and release from the pressures of the day".

Resveratrol as a diabetes drug has received quite a bit of research attention in recent years, particularly for type 2. (It is likely that the first resveratrol formulation released by Sirtris will be for type 2 diabetes.) With type 2, or non insulin-dependent diabetes, the problem isn't lack of insulin but rather the body is resistant to its effects. A study from the Kyung Hee University in South Korea helped to show how resveratrol works to overcome this insulin resistance. Normally, insulin activates an enzyme called AMP kinase which helps transport the glucose molecule into the cell, where it is put to use for stoking the metabolic machinery. Resveratrol is able to activate AMP kinase without insulin, and accentuate the activity of insulin when it is present.

Scientists have a way of studying diabetes in rats, by treating them with a chemical that kills off the cells that make insulin. (I can't imagine the hassles involved in giving them insulin injections but more difficult things have been done in the name of science.) In a study from Taiwan, diabetic rats were given resveratrol orally with meals in order to see whether blood sugar levels could be controlled. Resveratrol was found to be quite effective at reducing blood sugar levels, in both diabetic and nondiabetic rats. This latter finding is interesting, and the ability of resveratrol to prevent spiking blood sugar after meals may help explain why wine drinkers are less likely to be overweight.

The long-term problem with diabetes is effects on several organ systems; diabetics don't typically succumb to the direct effects of high blood sugar, but rather to vascular or neurological disorders. We know that wine, and resveratrol to some degree of specificity helps slow the progression of blood vessel disease. But one of the more intractable problems is the effect of diabetes on nerve cells. Diabetics often suffer from hypersensitivity to temperature, or loss of sensation in their extremities. Several recent studies point to a protective effect of resveratrol on this condition. Representative of these is a report from the National Institute of Pharmaceutical Education and Research in Punjab, India. Again using diabetic rats, they measured nerve impulse conduction and temperature sensitivity, finding significant improvement after a 2-week course of resveratrol. Another study from Spain found that resveratrol protects against oxidative stress in the brain of diabetic rats, and momentum is building around the whole topic. Expect to hear a lot more about resveratrol and diabetes.

Some wine with that joint? Resveratrol and arthritis

In chapter 3 we learned about the positive effects of alcohol on arthritis, but there is good reason to take it in the form of wine. Researchers in China, Germany, Turkey, and the U.S. have found dramatic benefits to resveratrol in experimental models of various types of arthritis, and they have been successfully untangling the way it works. At a basic level, arthritis is a condition marked by inflammatory destruction of the cartilage which forms the normally smooth surfaces of joints. This attack involves chemical messengers that give cells instructions to manufacture the substances involved in this self-directed chemical warfare. Some of the most successful drugs against arthritis work by ramping down the immune system by targeting these chemical messengers. Several labs have now found that resveratrol prevents most of the destruction of cartilage, at least in the lab. But importantly, it works at a direct molecular level so the immune system should be still able to function normally. (Much remains to be done here though, and there are no clinical trials to suggest that resveratrol supplements in oral form have a meaningful effect.)

Wine and Women

> *"Who loves not wine, women, and song remains a fool his whole life long."*
>
> —J.H. Voss

Wine has often been described in the same terms as one might rhapsodize about a beautiful woman: great legs,* nice body, etc. ... But this masculine-oriented view obscures the fact that a growing number of women are making their mark in the wine business. In the Sumerian *Epic of Gilgamesh*, one of the oldest poems known, a close relationship between women and winemaking is recounted. It is even possible that it was a woman who discovered wine in the first place: In ancient Persia, during the reign of Kind Jamshíd, a story is told that grapes were ordered to be stored in jars so that they would be available whenever the king desired. When some of the grapes became macerated and lost their sweetness, he imagined them to be poisoned and had the jar labeled as such. One of the women in his harem apparently suffered from chronic headaches so severe that she took the "poison"

---

* "Legs" are the streaks that run down the sides of the wine glass after the glass is tilted to coat the surface. They indicate the glycerol level, and give clues about the body and mouth feel of the wine.

in a suicide attempt. Overcome, she fell asleep but awoke refreshed and cured. (Again we see the restorative properties of wine intertwined with its origin stories.)

In any case, women and wine has long been a beautiful relationship, the chemistry of which is made more secure by resveratrol, and more complicated by alcohol. Resveratrol is a sort of natural estrogen, which is an unmitigated blessing in many ways, but alcohol remains a wild card, mired in the breast cancer risk dilemma. We will get into that in Chapter 7, but for now suffice it to say that for women who drink, red wine should be the default choice.

Regardless, the J-shaped curve is narrower and shallower for women, with optimal consumption at 1-2 glasses per day, as compared to 2-3 for men. It's a simple matter of physiology, like it or not. Women metabolize alcohol at a slower rate so the potential for harm enters the picture earlier. But the enduring controversy about alcohol and breast cancer has overshadowed an emerging line of research on some fairly unique ways that wine might benefit women. It's still a somewhat treacherous topic, but in many ways wine might turn out to be better for women than men. On average, women outlive men, in part because cardiovascular risk is pushed back beyond menopause to some extent. I should point out that the role of female hormones (estrogen, progesterone, and others) and heart disease is still not fully understood, however, and with this topic we are wading into an area of very dynamic debate and earnest research.

What makes resveratrol of particular interest is the similarity of one of its isomers to the hormone estrogen. Some studies have shown an estrogen-like effect, with a decrease in "hot flashes" and other peri-menopausal symptoms in women given resveratrol in amount equivalent to 2 glasses of red wine per day.* Resveratrol appears to also stimulate

---

* Women's health specialists uniformly caution against alcohol consumption during periods of rapid hormonal fluctuation, so considerable prudence is to be applied.

the bone cells that deposit calcium, thereby reversing osteoporosis, a process that may be attributable to its estrogen-like effects. Other polyphenols, notably a category known as *isoflavones* from soybeans show a similar effect. This phenomenon of ingested substances acting as hormones is known as *xenohormosis*, and is only beginning to be studied in detail.

A closer look at resveratrol's molecular structure reveals that its closest hormonal cousin is actually the synthetic estrogen *diethylstilbestrol* (DES). If this sounds familiar, you may recall that it was the first synthetic estrogen developed and widely prescribed in the 1950's and 60's to prevent miscarriages. It turned out to be not particularly effective, but it was eventually recognized that daughters of women who had used it during pregnancy were prone to a rare form of vaginal cancer, leading to its withdrawal from the U.S. market in 1971. Since there is some evidence that resveratrol has xeno-hormonal activity, caution seems advisable until more is known, at least for the massive doses that appear to be required in order to achieve the sirtuin activation effect in mammals. However, doses correlating to healthy wine consumption likely pose no risk.

It really boils down to this: estrogen and phytoestrogens protect to a degree against many degenerative conditions in women, including osteoporosis and of course cardiovascular disease. But the risk of breast and endometrial cancer is likely to be increased to a degree. I say "likely to be" because recommendations have been in a state of flux following a series of reports from a project known as the Women's Health Initiative, a sort of Framingham designed to asses the risks and benefits of postmenopausal hormone replacement therapy, or HRT. Further complicating (but hopefully clarifying the picture at some point) is the increasing use of phytoestrogens, among which are red wine polyphenols (especially resveratrol.) This would be of obvious interest I would think to men considering taking resveratrol supplements as well.

Resveratrol

DES

But first a little background on the Women's Health Initiative, and why it is so difficult to sort out the issues surrounding HRT. The primary health benefits of estrogen are protection against cardiovascular disease and osteoporosis, while the potential risks include the aforementioned higher incidence of breast and endometrial cancer, and blood clots. The project was a cohort study involving nearly 162,000 women, who were given either estrogen, a combination of estrogen and progesterone, or placebo. (Other variables including a low-fat diet, calcium supplementation, and vitamin D were also studied.) In February of 2004, the National Institutes of Health abruptly discontinued the study, causing widespread confusion and consternation. Many women on HRT panicked, and their doctors were sometimes equally at odds as to what to advise.

Why all the alarm? Although there were no changes in coronary disease or breast cancer, and in fact a lowered risk of hip fractures from osteoporosis, there was a slight increase in the risk of stroke and "mild cognitive impairment" in the estrogen-progesterone treatment group. These things are of course nearly impossible to measure with the degree of confidence that one would like. A reason for this is that the actions of estrogen hormones in the body aren't a simple "on/off" switch; there are at least three types of estrogen receptors, two inside the cell and one on the surface, and each responds differently when engaged by the hormone molecule. So in theory, if one could find something that hit the right balance of stimulating these receptors, the risks could be minimized while maximizing benefits.

The interactions of resveratrol with estrogen receptors are still being deciphered, but it does appear that the effects on each receptor type are different. It is entirely possible that it hits all the right notes, but the full score hasn't yet been written. The evidence does indicate a degree of protection against osteoporosis, and the well-established lower risk of cardiovascular disease among wine drinkers may or may not have much to do with resveratrol's estrogen-like behavior. Any increased risk of blood clotting would appear to be offset, since resveratrol has anticoagulant properties, and the cancer question will be explored in detail in the next chapter. There is as yet no indication that resveratrol results in feminizing effects in men, thank goodness, though high-dose effects aren't known.

One of the more interesting possibilities, just starting to be investigated, is the potential for resveratrol to maintain youthful skin. Phytohormonal activity may be important in this regard, since estrogen is essential for maintenance of moisture and collagen levels in the skin, and it helps maintain healthy hair. Many of the visible signs of skin aging progress more rapidly after menopause in direct measure to diminishing estrogen. Polyphenols and other phytoestrogens (e.g., from soy) are being intensively studied as additives to skin care products, though resveratrol appears to be uniquely well-qualified.

Consider first that resveratrol is produced in the skin of the grape in response to environmental stress; for the grape, resveratrol's *raison d'etre* is skin care. In this role, it serves many functions; it is an effective antibiotic against the fungi, bacteria, and parasites that attack grapes, and has been found to be similarly effective against common pathogens in human skin. It is uniquely capable of protecting the skin against the effects of ultraviolet radiation, including sunburns (though it is not a sunscreen per se.) This has actually been tested in mice (I can't shake the image of mice in tiny tanning beds) and researchers were able to show that resveratrol is involved in facilitating cell response to stress by ratcheting down production of compounds associated with DNA mutations and skin cancer. Because of this ability, resveratrol and other small-molecule polyphenols help to mute the inflammatory response to sun over-exposure and other environmental stressors; this in turn nullifies a whole cascade of harmful reactions. Evidence is amassing that resveratrol may help prevent skin cancers, including the non-threatening basal cell type and the potentially lethal melanoma.

Resveratrol may be suffering from a different version of overexposure though. Expectations are obviously sky high for the longevity effect to pan out, with millions of dollars at stake. But on a more mundane level, it seems to be capable of doing so many things that some are asking whether it really does any of them especially well, like a handyman molecule rather than a master carpenter. The possibilities are nevertheless exciting, and we haven't even gotten to the really interesting parts yet.

Chapter 7

Beyond Wine:
How Polyphenols are Redefining Nutrition

Filmmaker Woody Allen released a movie called "Sleeper" in 1973, in which his character is cryogenically frozen and thawed 200 years in the future. One of the gags in the film is his discovery that scientists have by then determined that chocolate and smoking are good for you. As it turns out, it was only another 20 years or so that chocolate was in fact found to have high doses of beneficial polyphenols (though smoking still appears to be not so good.) Many connoisseurs laud the pairing of red wines such as Cabernet sauvignon with dark chocolate, and the combination works because they contain many of the same polyphenols, resulting in harmonious "flavor notes."

This observation has not escaped the notice of researchers and even the business community. Supplements of dark chocolate have been tested at some length, much of the research having been underwritten by chocolate companies.* Some of the findings are indeed surprising, much as the wine-health story. But cocoa is only one source in a family of foods rich in phenolics. Since it is impractical or inadvisable for many of us to drink wine on a daily basis, alternative dietary sources are needed.

---

* The Mars candy company has invested considerable resources to develop a cocoa polyphenol-based nutrition supplement, under the brand name CocoaVia. Mars has been increasing the flavonol content in other products as well including the popular Dove Bar.

Kudos for Cocoa

Probably the best studied cousin in the polyphenol family is cocoa. Unprocessed cocoa does indeed have impressive anti-oxidant capacity. We should note at the outset however that only dark chocolate contains meaningful amounts, and the addition of milk or butterfat (not to mention sugar) may more than cancel out any beneficial effects. Also, most milk chocolate and other cocoa-containing confections are modified by what is called "Dutch process" which uses alkali to remove the bitter-tasting polyphenols for better palatability. Cocoa as a nutrient is substantially different from chocolate as a confection, and in general the less it is processed the better it is in terms of health benefits.

Eat chocolate, cure diabetes?

One of the most surprising findings on our growing list of unexpected health benefits from polyphenols is the evidence indicating that they have a unique capability to enhance sensitivity to insulin, the main hormone responsible for regulating blood sugar levels. (Resveratrol may not be unique in this ability.) An interesting study from an Italian university was reported in the *American Journal of Clinical Nutrition* in March 2005. They gave groups of test subjects a daily bar of either dark chocolate (with polyphenols) or white chocolate (without) and measured insulin resistance (typical of adult-onset, or type 2 diabetes) and insulin sensitivity using standardized tests. The dark chocolate group experienced significant improvement in both parameters. Other studies have found a similar effect. (It is of course important to note that I am not suggesting that diabetics start eating chocolate bars instead of taking their medication! Dark chocolate without the sugar may however be of some benefit, a point to discuss with your doctor.)

As with wine, much of the early research on cocoa was in the area of cardiovascular health. Studies on cocoa polyphenols have unearthed additional findings that point the way to these agents, whether from chocolate, wine or another source as a dietary key to vascular health. One such observation arrives indirectly: It has long been known, for example, that blood pressure normally increases with age, but certain isolated populations have been identified where this doesn't seem to occur; this translates into correspondingly lower incidences of cardiovascular problems. It was assumed that these populations, from such places as the remote highlands of Papua New Guinea and the Kuna people from the jungles of Central America, shared a gene that allowed their arteries to remain supple well beyond the age when most begin to stiffen with atherosclerosis.

Closer observation, however, cast doubt on the genetic theory, since when members of these tribes moved to modernized areas the effect disappeared. So the search was redirected at environmental factors, with the only common denominator found among these groups from different parts of the world being that they all regularly drank a beverage made from unprocessed cocoa. (In some instances, the urban cohort consumed less fish, but differences in cocoa intake were much greater.) Several clinical trials have now confirmed the ability of cocoa flavonoids to lower blood pressure, and recent work provides an explanation of how this occurs.

Just say N-O to hypertension

Elevated blood pressure (hypertension) has more than one cause. The aforementioned hardening of the arteries is well-known, but sometimes it is due to constant contraction of the muscles within the artery wall, resulting in a narrowing of the blood vessel. Blood pressure can be altered by disrupting the chemical signaling system that tells these muscles to constrict, or by encouraging those that foster relaxation of the muscle and dilation of the artery. The key molecule in this interaction is called Nitric Oxide, or NO as chemists abbreviate it. One of the mechanisms by which polyphenols lower blood pressure is via what is called "up-regulation" of NO production, a phenomenon demonstrated in numerous studies. This provides one plausible explanation for the cocoa effect in the population studies and the clinical trials, and the enhancement of insulin sensitivity is believed to relate to this activity as well.

The NO effect is transient, however, and the theory needs to also explain why people who consume wine or dark chocolate regularly have lower incidences of atherosclerosis, which develops over a period of years. We know that alcohol has some contribution for wine drinkers, by improving the LDL/HDL cholesterol ratio, but the fact that it is also rare in cocoa eating tribes suggests that polyphenols have a specific role to play in this regard also. Many factors contribute to hardening of the arteries; atherosclerosis is the result of a dynamic biological condition, not simply a matter of sludge buildup in old pipes.

Once we recognize that cocoa phenolics are for the most part the same as those found in wine, it makes perfect sense that we should find all of the same mechanisms for cardiovascular health. It is important to confirm, however, and literature documenting cocoa's capabilities is beginning to accumulate. We again find protection against LDL cholesterol oxidation, increased HDL, and so forth. Added to what we know about polyphenols already, we begin to see the complete picture: the true heart-healthy diet builds around a glass of wine and some dark chocolate.

Polyphenols and cardiovascular health

Lower levels of oxidized LDL cholesterol

Protein binding of LDL molecule

Induction of protective heat shock proteins

Inhibition of endothelins

Reduction of ischemia-reperfusion injury

Lowered blood pressure via enhanced NO production

Less chronic inflammation

Adenosine production

Inhibition of blood clotting

Anyone who suffered from teenage acne, and was told to avoid chocolate, will be intrigued by new evidence of how cocoa polyphenols actually help make *healthy* skin. Not only is it beneficial for inflammatory conditions such as acne, but a 2006 report from researchers in Germany revealed the potential of dietary cocoa as a sort of sunscreen. In this case, rather than slathering on the cocoa butter as many of us did when we were young, the cocoa was consumed orally. They conducted a 3-month trial involving 24 women, divided into 2 groups: each drank a daily cup of cocoa with breakfast, but one was flavonoid-enhanced and the other was more like standard hot chocolate. The primary flavonoids were cocoa-derived catechin and epicatechin. (Importantly, they were engineered to taste similar, so neither group knew which they were getting; this is called a "blinded" study and helps eliminate bias.)

Several tests were conducted on each subject, including exposure to standardized doses of ultraviolet light, akin to the method for testing SPF in sunscreens. The flavonoid-enhanced subjects experienced significantly

Non-wine dietary sources of polyphenols

Blueberries

Cranberries

Blackberries

Raspberries

Currants

Pomegranates

White & green tea

Coffee

Açai berries

Dark chocolate

Oils (esp. olive, soybean)

Capers

less reddening of the skin, which showed that dietary polyphenols can actually be an effective sunscreen! Blood flow to the skin was also improved. Other sophisticated tests included precise measurements of skin thickness, hydration, and smoothness, all showing measurable improvement. (Perhaps a fitting footnote to this study is that the designer *Coco Chanel* is said to have popularized tanning in the first place.)

Totaling tea phenolics

There is less of a controversy brewing over the health properties of tea, which also has many of the same phenolics as wine. An "Asian paradox" has been suggested, though the data isn't quite as compelling as with wine and the French. But it isn't difficult to notice that the tannic pucker of tea is reminiscent of the sensory feel in the mouth of red wine or cranberry juice; again, in the main the very same polyphenols. As a general rule, less processed teas have higher amounts of polyphenols; white tea, the least processed, is ideal but expensive and harder to find, so green tea is the usual recommended source. Since one can't in good conscience have wine with every meal, an alternative such as tea with breakfast and lunch seems to be a very worthwhile concept.

Population studies on tea echo those on red wine. One well-designed study from the Netherlands showed that there is a direct correlation of tea intake and lower rates of heart disease, confirming other epidemiologic findings that drinking at least one cup of tea can cut heart disease risk by nearly half (similar to wine drinkers.) Tea polyphenols have been found to be at least 20 times more potent in terms of their overall antioxidant capacity than vitamin E, and up to 200 times more potent than vitamin C (depending upon the testing method). Many of the research papers on tea and degenerative diseases, in fact, show a remarkable symmetry with wine studies, an observation more than suggestive of the primacy of polyphenols in the anti-aging arena.

Coffee's polyphenol perks

Tea has been so extensively evaluated in terms of its polyphenols that until recently no one thought to look at coffee. As it turns out, coffee has respectable amounts as well, and in some estimates they are the primary source of antioxidants in the typical Western diet. The trick here is not to neutralize them with milkfats or offset any benefits with too much sugar. As with cocoa and tea, the unadulterated versions are best.

There is a growing body of scientific literature addressing the question of coffee's role in a healthy diet. A representative study hails from the University of Oslo, Norway, though the data is from a project called the Iowa Women's health Study. This ambitious prospective cohort project involved nearly 42,000 postmenopausal women aged 55-69 at enrollment and followed for 15 years. The Oslo analysis looked at incidences of degenerative diseases related to inflammatory (oxidative) stress by coffee consumption. A sort of lazy J-shaped curve emerged, with coffee drinkers who consumed 1-3 cups per day on average about 25% less likely to die of cardiovascular disease, but less of an effect at 4 cups or greater. For other inflammatory diseases, there was more of a typical dose-response curve, mortality risk dropping to about two thirds that of non coffee-drinkers with more than 4 cups daily. These findings were attributed to the anti-oxidant properties of coffee phenolics.

A group from the University of Minnesota probed the same data set from the Iowa Women's Health Study to see what role, if any, caffeine might have. In this case, they explored statistics regarding the onset of type 2 diabetes (see box on page 118 about cocoa and diabetes.) Overall, women who drank 6 or more cups per day were 22% less likely to become diabetic, and the effect held true for decaffeinated coffee as well. So the risk reduction was not related to caffeine, implicating by default the polyphenols.

Coffee phenolics are somewhat different than those found in tea and wine. The most active ones are *caffeic acid, chlorogenic acid*, and a family of molecules termed *guiacols*. They are moderately assertive antioxidants, about as potent as vitamin E, though some studies find them more powerful. Some coffee polyphenols have an interesting capability regarding the mechanism of how genes are switched on or off. One way to turn on a DNA switch, thereby activating a gene, is a process called "methylation" (Chapter 2.) Some forms of cancer are due in part to methylation of switches in certain critical DNA segments, and this can be replicated in a laboratory setting using cancer cell cultures. Caffeic and chlorogenic acids from coffee have been shown to inhibit methylation in breast cancer cells and others. The implication here is that coffee polyphenols, like those from red wine or tea, are more than mere antioxidants; they have complex biological personalities all their own. Recent publications indicate that the most potent phenolics from coffee derive not from the beans, but from the inedible parts of the whole coffee berry that surround them.

Pomegranates

It would be hard not to notice that pomegranates have become fashionable. Store shelves display an ever-increasing array of pomegranate juice concoctions, and pomegranate martinis along with a bewildering assortment of pomegranate-infused cocktails adorn the bar menus of trendy watering holes. But in this case, the adage "What's old is new again" applies with a twist: The notion of pomegranates in anti-aging themes is *really* old. Some scholars have even posited that in the biblical Garden of Eden, the fateful fruit was in fact a pomegranate, not an apple.

The Parable of Persephone and the Pomegranate

Pomegranates appear in Greek mythology as well. Legend has it that Hades, god of the underworld, abducted Persephone, a beautiful goddess and daughter of Zeus, absconding with her to the realm of the dead. There he tempted her with delectable pomegranate seeds, apparently both irresistible and supernaturally powerful, and she was thereby bound to him as his queen. But Persephone's mother, Demeter, was distraught at the loss of her daughter and her sorrow caused the earth to be infertile; eventually a deal was made allowing Persephone to remain in Hades during the Winter, and the arrival of each Spring has subsequently been heralded with Persephone's visitation to the living world. Mystical and miraculous healing properties have been attributed to pomegranates for millennia since.

Is the reputation of pomegranates justified? Pomegranate juice purveyors are eager to point out that it is a powerful natural antioxidant elixir. As is the case with coffee, though, it is distinctly different from wine and tea. Pomegranate juice contains its own unique family of phenolics, the patriarch of which is a category called *ellagitannins*. Nutritional supplements are often standardized to a certain percentage of *ellagic acid*, a particularly potent antioxidant. Some studies indicate that it exceeds wine phenolics in this regard, and I for one often rely on pomegranate juice where wine is inappropriate (a frequent occurrence for a practicing surgeon.)

There are some issues to consider, however. A fundamental concept of nutritional biology is *bioavailability*, the question of how much of a nutritionally active substance is absorbed into the body and delivered in meaningful amounts to the target tissue. For orally ingested foodstuffs, this requires that it survive breakdown by hydrochloric acid and digestive enzymes in the stomach, then be absorbed into the bloodstream from the intestine, filtered and modified by the liver, taxied along by proteins in the blood, then delivered into the tissues where it is supposed to do something in an active form and sufficient amounts. The very purpose of this elaborate system of digestive processing is to break things down into usable components, not let random molecules wander willy-nilly wherever they may. In the case of ellagitannins from pomegranate juice, studies suggest that they don't get past the bouncers at the digestive door all that often, fashionable or not.

What this means is that there is much that remains to be learned about how well pomegranate polyphenols (and others) are absorbed and how they work in the body. This concept of bioavailability is the key to understanding how not just pomegranate phenolics might or might not be helpful, but the same applies to every nutritional food component. Take the case of the cocoa studies: The fact that measurable effects in the skin were documented after oral ingestion proves that in this instance, something in the cocoa was absorbed and eventually deposited in the skin where some beneficial reaction occurred. Since wine and cocoa phenolics are of the same family, the same benefit may be expected and this is an active area of research. Variations in bioavailability are why antioxidant activity in the test tube isn't always the same as in the body.

126 Richard A. Baxter, M.D.

Despite indications that pomegranate polyphenols may not be well-absorbed, there are a few clinical studies suggesting that it may have measurable cardiovascular benefits. A 2001 study from Israel reported that subjects drinking 50 ml (about ¼ cup) of pomegranate juice daily for two weeks lowered their blood pressure by about 5%. They followed this with a 3-year study on patients with atherosclosis of the carotid artery, the main supplier to the brain and the source of most strokes. (The carotid makes a convenient research target because the plaques can be imaged noninvasively.) In the "control" group, atherosclerotic plaques increased in thickness, while in the consumers of pomegranate juice the plaques regressed by as much as 30% over the first year. The results remained unchanged over the subsequent two years. These types of clinical studies are extremely valuable, as they fulfill a key criterion of the skeptic's checklist. (More clinical studies with wine need to be done, though financial sponsorship of such a project would be problematic; if funded by the wine industry, many would dismiss the results as marketing propaganda, and government grants would be seen as encouraging alcohol consumption.)

So pomegranate juice seems an excellent option, though its calorie content from natural sugars is higher than dieters might desire. I often combine it with açai (ah-sigh) juice, made from a berry which grows on a type of palm tree in the Amazon basin. This is another apparently impressive source of antioxidants, though not particularly sweet,* so it combines well with pomegranate. Açai juice is increasingly available in supermarkets, but despite claims of its antioxidant prowess, published literature is scarce. It is primary constituents appear to be flavonoids in the anthocyanin and proanthocyanidin categories. Only small amounts of resveratrol are found in açai berries.

Once one starts to look for nutritionally significant polyphenols, they do seem to turn up just about everywhere. If you have ever been to South America, you probably won't remember seeing people munching on açai berries, but in Argentina and Paraguay a type of herbal tea called Yerba maté is ubiquitous. Maté has its own polyphenol profile, and impressive

---

*   Check to be sure that sweeteners have not been added, many mixed-flavor açai drinks have as many calories as pomegranate juice or more.

antioxidant activity. There is even one study showing that rabbits on a high-cholesterol diet had less of a propensity for atherosclerosis if they were also given maté.

So it turns out that polyphenols are really not that unique in nature. In fact, a wide variety of foods have a respectable phenolic content, mostly those with colors in the same palette as wine and pomegranate juice (e.g., blueberries, cranberries, and the like.) If the term "anth*ocyan*in" reminds you of an ink color for your printer, you are not too far off. But there are many branches in the polyphenol family tree. One particularly relevant source derives from the Mediterranean diet, a central component of which is olive oil. Though really only a cousin in the polyphenol lineage, a phenolic called *hydroxytyrosol* imbues olive oil. It is responsible for the peppery taste that characterizes extra virgin oils. Hydroxytyrosol is subject to breakdown at higher temperatures though, so it may be better for dressing a salad than sautéing. Or do as Jeanne Calment did: use olive oil as a moisturizer!

A particularly potent source of polyphenols is capers, another Mediterranean ingredient. (Capers are the immature flower buds of the caper plant, and contain the flavonoid *rutin* in addition to some of the same polyphenols found in red wine, in particular quercetin.) Some spices, notably *curcumin* (the stuff that makes curry yellow) have been evaluated in considerable detail with rewarding results. But the concentration of polyphenols in any given food material must be divided by whatever portion size is reasonable, in order to place it into its proper place in the diet; tablespoonfuls of curry powder or cups of capers might pack a polyphenol punch but there are more sensible strategies. A couple of glasses of wine with dinner, on the other hand, should definitely be doable.

A rational interpretation of all of this is to recognize that polyphenols are not all created equal, and labeling them all as "antioxidants" is an oversimplification. Not only do they have a long list of capabilities beyond free radical scavenging, but there are likely a variety of ways in which they interact with each other. The optimal combinations are probably unknowable with precision. An ever-growing parade of health beverages from exotic fruits already crowds store shelves, with dramatic claims of antioxidant potency. Usually, however, all that is disclosed is a number reflecting a particular measure of antioxidant prowess, and when compared to the thousands of research papers on wine, we should expect more.

Though we are just beginning to put together the pieces of the polyphenol puzzle, it is fair to say that polyphenols are redefining nutritional science. In the twentieth century, vitamins were the story; once they were discovered and their roles defined, we could rest comfortably knowing that beri-beri and rickets were things of the past. As with so many things, however, the law of unintended consequences introduced a darker side of vitamin science. Food production could now be industrialized, and marketed on the basis of convenience and added-in flavors. Traditional methods of growing and preparing food, based on accumulated wisdom of what is necessary for complete nutrition, were supplanted by more efficient means. The vitamins which had been stripped out by processing could be added back in later, along with sweeteners, modified fats (e.g., the malevolent trans-fats), and artificial coloring (this latter being necessary to disguise the lack of polyphenols, a fact not appreciated). Likewise, the tradition of wine with dinner could be disassembled into the component parts of drinking, to be reconstituted into cocktails unconnected with meals. Polyphenols once again made an exit.

We may credit the role of vitamins in sustaining the oxidative damage theory of aging though. The antioxidant vitamins (A,C, and E), tepid though they are in this regard, appeared to explain the anti-aging manifestations of vegetable-rich diets and kept the notion alive. It would only be a matter of time before the importance of polyphenols, from wine and other sources, was determined. What vitamins were to the last century, polyphenols are to the new one, bringing us back to the primary source. What we may lose in convenience in the struggle to recreate healthier ways of producing and preparing food, we gain in flavors and simple pleasures. Not that chocolate and wine could be considered any great sacrifice!

> *Nothing would be more tiresome than eating and drinking if*
> *God had not made them a pleasure as well as a necessity.*
> —Voltaire

Chapter 8

How Wine Fights Cancer

" ... for filled with that good gift, suffering mankind forgets its grief"

—Euripides (on wine)

At first glance the notion that red wine might be part of the solution to cancer prevention seems at the very least unlikely. Everything that has previously been believed about wine and cancer implied a *causal* relationship, not a *protective* one. Since many cancers are degenerative diseases, however—that is, related to age and environment—perhaps it should come as less of a surprise in view of the fact that many cases are linked to lifestyle factors and therefore preventable to some degree. This is heartening news since we typically think of cancer as a sort of random serial killer, striking without warning. Many types of cancers tragically do still fall into that category, but cancer, like a serial killer, often selects its victims based upon behaviors that put them in jeopardy. Certain activities increase risk of cancer, but the notion that we can actively lower risk has received less emphasis. It isn't simply a matter of *not* doing certain things (smoking, eating a high-fat diet) but also of proactively *doing* things, such as consuming foods with anti-cancer compounds, and yes, drinking wine. We are in fact not completely helpless to modify the odds of being stricken with cancer, and red wine may be one of our most effective tools.

Body of Data

Epidemiologists have identified many of the lifestyle factors that place us in peril, from smoking and sunburns to dietary habits. On the other hand, we are less likely to be struck with cancer if we eat a diet high in fiber and rich in vegetables (this was the data that inspired the trials of antioxidant vitamins.) And drink wine? The growing body of data about *wine* and cancer is at odds with many of the preconceptions about *alcohol* and cancer, once again challenging dogma. But we will see that wine not only lowers cancer risk in a statistical sense across the board, but specific wine-derived polyphenols block the progress of cancer at every turn. These substances, notably but not exclusively resveratrol, help protect cells against becoming cancerous in the first place, inhibit the growth of cancer cells when they do develop, and work to prevent cancer from spreading. (Some of them are even being investigated as possible chemotherapeutic agents.[*]) Preemptive blocking of cancer with targeted dietary constituents has even been given its own new word: *chemoprevention.*

As with heart disease, the indication had always been that alcohol was a risk factor for cancer. Some of the first clues that this may not be the case with all forms of alcohol came from Serge Renaud's work. In a 1999 report of a population study involving 36,000 healthy men in eastern France, the risk of dying of all causes was lower in moderate wine drinkers, confirming earlier studies. The lower rate of cardiovascular disease had seemed an adequate explanation. But this study also looked at specific causes of death, and found that men who drank one to three glasses of wine per day had a *cancer* death risk that was lower by around 20%. Morten Grønbaek, in a study published the following year reached the same conclusion, noting also that drinkers of spirits or beer had a

---

[*]   Polyphenols for chemotherapy have multiple potential advantages. One study of uterine and ovarian cancer cells found that resveratrol enhanced the effectiveness of the drugs cisplatin and doxorubicin while protecting against some of the most troublesome side-effects. Similar results have been reported for quercetin.

slightly *higher* risk. Surprisingly, even lung and throat cancer rates were lower among wine drinkers.

The reason this was unexpected is that throat cancer *does* have a statistically positive association with alcohol consumption. But this data had never before been analyzed looking for the possibility that the subcategory of moderate wine drinkers might be different. One thing that was known for sure is that heavy drinkers who also smoke do have a substantial increase in mouth and throat cancer; the risk seems to be multiplied by the combination rather than the sum of the two added together. But this category of individuals tend to be spirits drinkers rather than wine drinkers, and even drinking wine, if in excess, erases the benefits that are enjoyed with moderation. The principle of the J-shaped curve applies to cancer risk as it does for heart disease and all-cause mortality.

The European studies on wine and cancer stimulated interest worldwide, at least in the research community. One large and widely reported study came from the renowned Fred Hutchinson Cancer Research Center in Seattle in 2004. This was a case-control analysis of prostate cancer and alcohol consumption in middle-aged men. *Overall* alcohol consumption was discovered to be unrelated to prostate cancer, but there was a strong dose-response relationship between red wine consumption and *lowered* risk: For each glass of red wine consumed per week, the chance of having prostate cancer dropped 6%.

Other polyphenol vehicles get in on the act too. A report from the Department of Preventative Medicine at the University of Southern California School of Medicine related the low incidence of breast cancer in Japanese women to green tea consumption. A similar study from the Aichi Cancer Center in Nagoya, Japan demonstrated that increasing tea consumption correlated with lower stomach cancer risk, and coffee conferred a degree of protection from colon cancer.

Does alcohol increase the risk of breast cancer?

Where the question of wine and cancer most cuts across the grain, however, is with breast cancer. Epidemiologists have struggled with this issue for decades. Most studies have tended to show a positive but weak correlation between alcohol consumption and breast cancer, and any willingness by epidemiologists to embrace new findings about wine intake and health was tempered by these observations. It would be inappropriate to promulgate advice to imbibe if it simply meant a tradeoff between a benefit in one category and a detriment in another, just as jumping out of a burning building may save you from getting burned, but your odds of breaking a leg are undoubtedly higher. And since pre-menopausal women are at lower risk for heart disease than men of similar age, they would probably not gain much from moderate wine consumption in terms of cardiovascular health. (The number one killer of women is still heart disease, though, despite the attention that breast cancer commands as a women's issue.)

Data from the Nurses' Health Study[*] involving more than 85,000 women helps to shed some light on this. This project followed a female cohort for a period of 12 years beginning in 1980. In this population, light-to-moderate drinking was associated with lower mortality rates, primarily from reduced heart disease incidence. Heavier drinking, as one would predict from the J-shaped curve, had increased mortality; this was largely from an increased incidence breast cancer, in addition to more obvious sequelae of alcoholism such as liver cirrhosis. Overall, the benefits of moderate drinking appeared to be confined to heart disease. So the conclusion was that women should limit their alcohol consumption to no more than one drink per day, in order to balance an apparent trade-off between heart health and breast cancer. But remember, overall *alcohol* consumption isn't necessarily the same as *wine* drinking.

Meta-analysis: The rising tide

The evidence that alcohol increases breast cancer risk seemed to be mounting on a gradually rising tide of research data. By the mid-1990's, more than three dozen epidemiologic studies had been published. A meta-analysis was compiled by Dr. Matthew Longnecker of the UCLA

---

[*]   Recall this was the study coordinated by the Harvard School of Public Health and 6 hospitals in the Boston area.

School of Public Health in 1993. Dr. Longnecker evaluated 38 studies, 10 of the population type and 28 case-control reports. By combining the results, an apparent "dose-response curve" was created that indicated that moderate alcohol consumption increased breast cancer risk by about 10%. Larger intakes increased the risk further, reinforcing the conclusion of a cause-effect relationship. One daily drink produced an increased risk of 10%, two drinks 20%, and so forth.

When the studies are compounded, however, certain problems with the data become magnified as well. For one, not all studies found a positive correlation between alcohol and breast cancer. Of the 38 studies in the UCLA meta-analysis, three found an *inverse* correlation and 20 found a statistically insignificant association, casting a shadow of doubt on inferences about a possible link. What's more, among the studies with the longest follow-up the correlation was weakest. So despite the magnitude gained by massing the studies together, evidence of a link between low-to-moderate alcohol consumption and breast cancer remained lukewarm. While higher levels of consumption were more clearly linked to breast cancer, at low levels it is more a matter of extrapolation rather than direct evidence.

There are other problems with the data. For example, there is a wide variability between different countries and different drinking patterns. Stratification for confounding variables such as diet and smoking habits is not always thorough. And of importance to the topic of wine and cancer, most of the studies tended to consider alcohol from all sources together, making it difficult to extract the data about wine specifically. If wine has substances that are *beneficial* in terms of breast cancer risk, this positive effect could be obscured by the alcohol-cancer link, particularly at moderate levels.

Is alcohol a carcinogen?

Adding to the debate is the fact that a plausible biological mechanism by which alcohol might trigger malignant change in breast tissue has not been put forth. Various theories have been proposed but none have been supported with direct scientific evidence. We do know that alcohol is a pro-oxidant, and it may be correctly classified as a co-carcinogen on that basis. But alcohol has never been shown to be a carcinogen by itself, in breast tissue or other types of cells, despite its statistical connection in epidemiological surveys. Some studies have suggested that women on hormone supplements are at increased sensitivity to alcohol-provoked carcinogenesis, but this is an inconsistent finding and remains conjecture. As we established with the skeptic's checklist, epidemiologic findings without the foundation of a plausible biologic explanation, supported by objective research, must remain open to question.

Just as it would be reckless to recommend wine on a nutritional basis without a complete foundation of independently verified research, it is also dubious to promulgate policy based on inconsistent data and incomplete understanding. Given the variability of the results from surveys on alcohol and breast cancer, it is fair to say that a question mark remains, at least for low-to-moderate levels of *wine* consumption. The pattern seems to imply an overall risk of alcohol with breast cancer, with increasing risk linked to higher intakes, but certain assumptions are required to assign this risk to wine consumption at low levels. And we know that wine is not the same as spirits or beer where other health issues are concerned, so why would it not be different with breast cancer?

Back to Framingham

It seems somehow fitting that the Framingham data should bookend our discussion of the breast cancer-alcohol question. A 1999 report revisited the original cohort as well as the offspring cohort, with specific reference to alcohol and breast cancer. Although this study population is not the largest, it produces some of the most reliable data due to the rigorous study design and the length of the study. The 1999 report included follow-up of more than forty years in the original cohort and over twenty years in the offspring group. In the wake of the critical fallout after the government's earlier attempts to censor "undesirable" Framingham data, the scientists in control of the project were subsequently able to assert greater academic freedom and thereby establish greater credibility to their findings. This study found no association of any type of alcoholic beverage at light-to-moderate levels with breast cancer.

The breast news yet?

Not long after I finished this chapter, another major review came out looking at the alcohol/cancer question. It was reported by Arthur Klatsky at the European Cancer Conference in September of 2007. The big news was that, after careful analysis of the most recent data, even wine drinkers were at risk with as little as a glass a day. Coming from such a preeminent source, the conclusion resulted in widespread consternation and a degree of concern that perhaps wine wasn't so privileged after all in the cancer risk calculation.

In order to gain some perspective, it is helpful to ask why there are so many studies on alcohol and breast cancer in the first place. Clearly, they should have been able to sort all of this out by now, and Klatsky's review was widely interpreted as the definitive word. But one reason researchers keep coming back to the topic is that the results from the studies are so highly variable. Almost at the same time Dr Klatsky was speaking in Barcelona, another meta-analysis in Japan was published. Their conclusion? "…epidemiologic evidence on the association between alcohol drinking and breast cancer risk remains insufficient …"

We may never get the real answer about the risks of low-to-moderate wine drinking and breast cancer for a simple reason: for the most part, suitable study populations don't exist anymore. What I mean by this is that population studies are a sort of experiment, except that instead of assigning different groups to different interventions (e.g., new drug vs. placebo) we are looking for population segments that have naturally sorted themselves into different lifestyles. In more traditional times, a consistent way of living throughout life defined certain communities; one could realistically believe that people who drink red wine with meals did so on a regular basis and didn't drink much else. Now, even those who report that they have a glass or two of wine with dinner might well also go out for margaritas on Friday night and have a beer on Saturday, or drink differently in different seasons. The prime opportunities for this type of research passed a generation ago.

And still missing is an evidence-supported theory of exactly how alcohol works as a carcinogen.

A May 2008 study from southern France helped to clarify the picture somewhat. This was a case-control study with 437 breast cancer cases, with the finding that at low levels (less than 1.5 drinks per day) of any type of alcohol consumption, breast cancer risk was lower; this was attributed to that fact that most alcohol consumption in this population was wine. With increased levels of drinking, wine conferred a more obvious benefit as compared to other libations; in other words, there was a J-shaped curve! What is of further interest is that patterns of drinking seemed to be important for any type of alcohol: the lowest risk was for regular drinking in moderate amounts as opposed to weekend binging, for example.

This highlights the fact that even a low level of risk would need to be balanced against the known benefits of sensible wine drinking. The most generous interpretation of the alcohol-cancer data implies an increased chance of developing breast cancer in the 10-30% range, in post-menopausal women. But measured against decreased odds of heart attack and stroke in the range of 30-40%, and potential benefits in terms of diabetes, osteoporosis, gallstones, and Alzheimer's disease, a substantial net gain in overall survival and general health is still evident. This is precisely why a broader view is needed; the temptation is to consider each disease risk profile in isolation, or to look only at the risk side of the ledger while maintaining a blind spot for the benefit side.

Vitamin benign

Environmental factors other than alcohol habits may provide some clues about the variability of the data, as well as how risk can be modified to advantage. Dietary factors have long been suspect in terms of breast cancer, though the precise elements in various diets have eluded identification. A study of nearly 57,000 women in the Canadian National Breast Screening Study, published in 2000 from the University of Toronto evaluated the role of dietary folate (vitamin B-9). Folate is required for optimal DNA repair, which as we know is needed on an ongoing basis due to damage from environmental oxidative stress. Alcohol interferes with folate metabolism, which may in part explain its association with various cancers. Inadequate availability of folate increases the odds of a cancerous mutation in DNA.

At low levels of alcohol consumption, one or two glasses of wine per day, dietary folate did not seem to make a difference in this group with such a small incidence of breast cancer. That is likely due to that fact that it is statistically impossible to measure improvements in risk where the risk is minimal to begin with. But at higher levels of alcohol consumption, the role of dietary folate emerged as a critical factor, especially in postmenopausal women. The fact that heavy drinkers also tend to have poor nutritional habits probably amplifies the effect. So whatever increased risk there may be with alcohol from any source, it appears that it can be overcome to a significant extent simply by eating a healthy diet with adequate B vitamins.

It's the polyphenols

The question of a protective role of polyphenols could not be answered by this type of study, though it was a subject of growing interest in France and elsewhere. Techniques for isolating and purifying polyphenol extracts from red wine were being improved. It was known that polyphenols could inhibit the growth of cancer cells in a test tube, but could levels corresponding to moderate drinking have a clinical effect? Just about anything in high enough concentration could kill cells in culture, so if wine polyphenols are the key they need to have an effect at concentrations achievable in a healthy wine diet.

A Greek scientist, Elias Castanas M.D., Ph.D., provided the answer in a breakthrough study. Not surprisingly, given the context of biased attitudes about wine and cancer, two scientific journals reportedly refused to publish his findings despite careful research methodology.

The study was eventually published in the *Journal of Cellular Biochemistry*, a well-established peer-reviewed scientific reference, in June of 2000.

Dr. Castanas employed a commonly used method involving cancer cell cultures. Basically, this technique tests the effect of various substances on the proliferation of cancer cells kept alive in a laboratory. Since alcohol is toxic to any cells in cultures of this type, he used only purified polyphenol extracts from Cabernet Sauvignon wine. The polyphenols catechin, epicatechin, quercetin, and resveratrol, as well as the total polyphenol extract were tested against three separate breast cancer cell cultures. In each case, strong inhibition was observed even at very low concentrations. The results were so dramatic that the tests were repeated several times to make sure the findings were real.

Not content with this observation, the researchers tested various models to explain the findings. Two of the breast cancer lines were of a type known as hormone-sensitive; that is, natural hormones such as estrogen accelerate tumor growth with these cancers. Polyphenols were found to interfere with this process by binding the estrogen receptors on the surface of the cancer cells via a protein binding mechanism. It's a sort of molecular "musical chairs" leaving the estrogen molecules standing around. Without their hormone stimulus, the cancer cells are literally fooled into shifting into a more senescent state.

But protein binding of hormone receptors was not enough to explain the findings by itself, and the non-hormone sensitive cell lines were also suppressed in equal measure. So the researchers evaluated the effect of oxidative stress using a technique that exposed the cells to free radicals. The potent anti-oxidant properties of the polyphenols were found to exert a strongly protective effect at low concentrations by at least two different means.

Encouraged by their findings with breast cancer cells, they tested the cabernet polyphenols against prostate cancer cultures also. Again a dose-dependent inhibition was found, with resveratrol the most potent. In this model, the effect was found to be due to modulation of nitric oxide (NO) production, in concentrations equating to moderate wine consumption. This test also used different cancer cell lines, of the hormone-sensitive and non-sensitive types, with positive results in every case.

We now have evidence that wine does much more than act as a safety lock on the oxidation trigger. This is important, because it takes more than one episode of oxidative stress to convert an otherwise law-abiding cell into a full-fledged malignant outlaw. Researchers who study the ways in which cells begin to misbehave and descend into malignancy divide the process into three steps: *initiation, promotion,* and *progression.* Several factors are involved in each of these steps, and wine polyphenols have a specific role in policing each of them.

The polyphenol that has received the most attention in cancer prevention is resveratrol. Research teams at the University of Chicago and the University of Illinois have investigated the actions of resveratrol in each of these steps, and in each case it has been found to have dramatically impressive effects. Considering that resveratrol and other polyphenols exist in plants in order to protect the plant from viral, fungal, and parasitic infestation, as well as oxidative damage from solar radiation and other environmental stresses, it makes sense that they should protect animal DNA in similar ways.

Initiation, the first step toward malignancy, refers to the sequence of events that culminate in a mutation in a critical gene. Resveratrol, like other potent antioxidants, helps prevent the DNA damage in the first place by neutralizing the free radicals that corrode the DNA. The Chicago group provided confirmation of Castanas' findings in a study using prostate cancer cells. Even when chemicals were added that promote free radical production, resveratrol provided protection.

There is another somewhat surprising effect of resveratrol that relates to its ability to suppress the COX (cyclo-oxygenase) enzyme system. COX enzymes have been thought to be primarily involved in cardiovascular health (Chapter 3), and generalized inflammation-related aging, but they appear to play a vital role in cancer in specific ways. COX enzymes are implicated in activation of carcinogens, and they appear to be at the scene of the cancer crime with regularity. Certain substances known to cause mutations in DNA are unable to get at the core genetic material without activation by COX, so resveratrol helps by blocking this key step. It's like taking the car keys from someone who's had too much.

All of the common anti-inflammatory medications work by COX inhibition. Aspirin, ibuprofen, and the whole class of drugs called "non-steroidal anti-inflammatory drugs" or NSAIDS, are capable of COX inhibition. In fact, evidence exists that some NSAIDS are themselves able to directly disrupt carcinogenesis by this means. There are two known forms of COX, called (not surprisingly) COX-1 and COX-2. The primary form of COX is the one involved in blood clotting and inflammation, while COX-2 is seen more rarely but might be more important in cancer transformation.

This is an important distinction because resveratrol inhibits both forms* while most NSAIDS affect primarily COX-1. Nearly every type of cancer studied has been found to have elevated levels of COX-2, and substances known to inhibit the enzyme appear to hold great promise in reducing cancer risk and cancer survival. (There are some 900 published papers on COX-2 and cancer.) So again we come back to the unique role of wine polyphenols.

But resveratrol worked in other ways to suppress initiation, by blocking one of the pathways that lead to free radical production before they have a chance to attack. This was demonstrated in two different studies. The first one used a culture of pre-leukemia cancer cells, which were exposed to known carcinogens with and without resveratrol present. Resveratrol was able to prevent the formation of the free radicals that cause the malignant change, thereby disarming the carcinogens and halting the malignant conversion before it even started.

Of course it doesn't stop there. Allowing a mutation to go unrepaired is not always enough to corrupt a cell into becoming a malignant threat. A conspiracy of certain conditions is required in order for a cell with damaged DNA to begin its chaotic rampage. These circumstances define the second stage, which researchers call *promotion*. If the promotion phase can be arrested, there may still time to rally the troops of the body's immune defenses and turn the nascent tumor back.

Anti-promotion activity can also be measured in several ways. One of the more significant conditions that enable promotion has to do with

---

* Since NSAID's are most commonly used as analgesics, it makes sense that other COX enzyme inhibitors may work the same way. It has been proposed that resveratrol has analgesic properties and is being investigated for that use.

inflammation, also mediated by COX enzymes. As we know resveratrol is a strong anti-inflammatory and so has a major impact on this process. Another mouse model, using cells called "fibroblasts," was used to test the anti-promotion phase more specifically, and again resveratrol was found to be protective in conditions otherwise tolerant of unrestricted cell growth. If anti-initiation activity is analogous to taking the keys away from a drunk, anti-promotion is more like disabling the car's engine just in case.

Once a tumor gets its foot in the door, the third phase—progression—is where it sets up housekeeping and really begins to take over. This brings us to one of the most exciting areas of wine polyphenol research. The idea that wine-derived polyphenols can evict cancer even after it has begun to grow roots is one of the most unexpected revelations yet. Evidence for this comes from at least one study demonstrating that leukemia cells could be persuaded to revert back to a benign state by resveratrol. To continue our analogy, it's like apprehending the lawbreaking cells even after they've started to drive away.

Polyphenol activity in tumors is being deciphered in detail. Cancer cells, like normal cells, require an elaborate communication system of message molecules carrying signals for various sustaining chemical processes. In the normal course of an organism's existence, certain cells become unnecessary and auto-destruct; this is known as "apoptosis." Cancer cells have typically developed ways to bypass apoptosis signals, usually by disabling the gene that codes for the protein messenger molecules. One of the ways that wine phenolics (primarily resveratrol) impact cancerous behavior is by promoting apoptosis via modulation of these signals; they actually trick the cells into committing suicide. Cells also need a way to abort the self-destruct sequence, and so there are "anti-apoptotic" proteins too; in this case, polyphenols block them and thereby prevent an end-run.

Resveratrol is not the only anti-cancer polyphenol, though, even if it has received the most attention. In some models, quercetin has been more effective, while others get the best results with the total polyphenol extract. It would be premature to give credit for wine's anti-cancer properties to a single molecule; recall how promising beta-carotene appeared to be as a chemoprotective agent. It was fifteen years before we found out that it only worked in a natural dietary context, and by virtue of something else (polyphenols). Resveratrol in pill form is already widely marketed, but experience suggests that the maximum benefit will be in red wine. A study from the School of Medicine at the University of Puerto Rico found convincing evidence to support that view. In a series of interesting experiments involving breast cancer cell cultures, they showed that the combination of the polyphenols resveratrol, quercetin, and catechin at doses corresponding to healthy wine consumption was a more effective inhibitor than high doses of any individual one.

The lifestyle ledger

Unlike many other environmental and dietary factors, we now have epidemiologic evidence that red wine reduces cancer risk, confirmed with independent studies and supported by a foundation of laboratory research that demonstrates a plausible basis for the effect. But it can still be a long road from the laboratory to public policy, and we need to weigh the results of clinical trials. What seems compelling in a laboratory experiment may not translate into worthwhile clinical strategies. We have new and exciting possibilities before us, but we have only just opened the door.

Even the best surveillance systems and security guards let the occasional criminal get away though, so wine polyphenols appear to reduce cancer risk by a maximum of about twenty percent. But considering the millions of cases of cancer each year, adopting healthy wine drinking habits could save millions of lives, not to mention pain and suffering. There are more than half a million cancer deaths in the United States each year; a twenty per cent reduction is over one hundred thousand lives that could be saved simply by having wine with dinner.

Nevertheless, there continues to be considerable unease about the subject of wine and cancer, regardless of the increasingly persuasive data. Perhaps this is because many are still uncomfortable with the idea that alcohol remains part of the formula. It is human nature to want to define threats to our health in absolute terms rather than statistical

Thirteen anti-cancer properties of wine polyphenols

Anti-initiation

Antioxidant

Anti-mutation

Prevention of carcinogen activation

Anti-promotion

Inhibition of COX-2

Induction of apoptosis (cancer cell "auto-destruct")

Decreased expression of anti-apoptotic proteins

Down-regulation of cell "activation pathways"*

Anti-progression

Suppressed growth factor signaling pathways

Prevention of cancer cell invasion

Suppression of cancer cell growth

Suppression of angiogenesis (formation new blood vessels required for tumor growth)

Enhanced therapy

Improved effectiveness of chemotherapeutic agents

Enhanced response to radiation treatment, decreased side-effects

* For the scientifically conversant, these are: NF-κB, AP-1, JAK-STAT, and others.

probabilities. Ultimately, the question of wine and cancer, or any other lifestyle factor, is a net sum game. If we look only at data that seems to imply that alcohol increases breast cancer risk, it is reasonable to conclude that it is unwise to endorse any level of alcohol consumption. Yet when we remove wine from the lifestyle ledger, we automatically "dial in" higher risk of heart disease, stroke, osteoporosis, etc., and we lose the wine-specific polyphenol assets. Deaths and disease sustain a substantial net increase.

Likewise, if we add polyphenols in isolation (for, example as a supplement pill) we add in several unknowns; balance determines the most sensible approach. Moderation in all aspects of diet and lifestyle universally defines the lowest risk category, with cancer as with heart disease and other degenerative conditions. Living a full and rewarding life is certainly more than simply the absence of disease, however, so wine with dinner can be both a simple pleasure and a common-sense strategy.

Chapter 9

Ideal for the Old:
How Wine Protects the Brain

"... ideal for ... the old ... and for anyone who needs to use their brain."
>   —Dr. Robert Druitt, 1873, on the effects of wine

Simply growing old is not as daunting as the specter of losing one's faculties and the ability to enjoy meaningful interactions with family and friends. It is often said that good wine improves with age, though of course not always; aging wine to its apogee of quality is pointless unless it is shared anyway. But perhaps the most surprising effect of regular, moderate wine drinking is the revelation that mental function is *enhanced*, not only in youth, but also as the brain ages. The very notion of "prescribing" wine for the elderly seems nonsensical, conjuring up visages of nursing homes filled with belligerent drunkards. Wouldn't it be logical to assume that since alcohol is toxic to brain cells, any form of drinking would be harmful, especially for the elderly? Can it be true that the opposite is the case?

The question is one of greater importance than it might seem at first glance. Alzheimer's disease, and other forms of senile dementia (for purposes of our discussion here one and the same, though there are important distinctions) affect some four million Americans already. Up to half of those older than 85 are affected to some degree, and the numbers are expected to increase drastically in the coming years.

The costs of Alzheimer's to society are almost incalculable; care of these patients has presently been estimated to run $100 billion annually, with another $60 billion or so in lost productivity as family members take time away from work for care of affected relatives.

Even milder forms of cognitive impairment, especially when associated with other degenerative medical conditions, contribute to earlier need for assisted living and even institutionalization. As the "baby boom" generation reaches their sunset years, the already burgeoning healthcare costs will swell in tsunami proportions from the additional burden of cognitive disorders. The true costs are almost too staggering to contemplate, so any intervention that helps to prevent age-related cognitive decline deserves a look. Even a small improvement could save billions of dollars, not to mention quality of life issues. So if a daily dose of wine can lower the risk at all, the possibility merits investigation.

As with the issue of wine and cardiovascular health, and cancer, acceptance of the discovery that wine *protects* the brain has been an uphill battle. It should come as no surprise by now, however–based on what we know about wine phenolics in other aspects of health–that long-held assumptions and attitudes about drinking and thinking were at least partly wrong. Because alcohol is toxic to nerve cells, chronic alcohol consumption in excess does lead to irreversible neurological decline. But as with other measures, what is true for moderation is not true for either abstinence or excess. Once again it is *wine* that holds the key, especially when it is part of a lifelong pattern.

Vascular disease and brain function

Before examining the epidemiological data, it will be helpful to remember that in general, what is good for the heart is good for the brain. The very act of conscious thought requires an enormous expenditure of metabolic energy which in turn needs a constant supply of oxygen-rich blood. Since alcohol (and more specifically wine) helps ensure clean arteries and good blood flow to the heart muscle, the brain must be getting better blood too. That is no doubt why the most common type of stroke—the type due to blood clots blocking blood flow to the brain—is less common in parallel measure to the reduction in heart attack risk among moderate wine drinkers.

The brain is not only more metabolically demanding than the heart, it is also more massive. This in turn requires an elaborate network of tiny capillaries in order to ensure a robust percolation of oxygen into every nook and cranny of the gray matter. However, it doesn't take much to begin plugging up these micro-vessels, rendering the brain cells they feed vulnerable. In many cases, mental decline with advancing age is attributable to the "micro-strokes" caused by deterioration in the microcirculation. Typically, these strokes are so small that they are scarcely noticed, but as they accumulate over time the brain loses processing power.

One way to minimize this slow accumulation of sludge in the microcirculation is with anticoagulants. We know of course that aspirin, alcohol, and wine polyphenols can help in this regard, as well as herbal blood thinners such as the popular supplement *Ginkgo biloba*. However, results from clinical studies on anticoagulants are highly variable where they relate to memory or other measures of cognition. Keep in mind also that short-term memory is only one measure of brain function and, by inference, micro-circulation. Anticoagulants, regardless of variety, don't appear to be up to doing the job of protecting the brain alone.

There are at least two explanations for the inconsistent evidence about anticoagulants and brain function. One would expect any anticoagulant, regardless of source, to show a benefit primarily in those with established vascular disease, but not those with normal healthy arteries. The clots that shower into the brain's microcirculation originate from plaques in the larger arteries, so anything that prevents these clots from forming might show a relatively acute effect in those with atherosclerosis. But no measurable change would be expected in those without pre-existing disease, since there is no sludge buildup to retard blood flow or initiate clot formation in the first place. Another reason is that any influence of anticoagulation that *prevents* slow deterioration would take years to produce a measurable change. Since we are looking for slower than expected rate of decline—as opposed to immediate improvement of function—the ability to evaluate such a difference would require a large scale, long-term, and ultimately impractical study.

Drink for Thought

Wine drinkers may believe they are smarter, others may dismiss the notion as elitist pretension, but there is actually some evidence of a correlation between IQ and preference for wine. The data comes from one of Grønbaek's projects at Copenhagen University, published in 2004. In Denmark, all men at age 18 must register for the military draft and undergo evaluation, including physical examination and intelligence testing. The study was originally intended to compare IQ with other factors known to have health consequences, specifically obesity and alcohol abuse, but it provided an insight into wine drinking as well.

The study was essentially a cohort analysis, in which a randomly selected population group was evaluated between 1981 and 1983, and again in 1992-94, and the results were then tabulated according to their baseline evaluations at the time of their draft board registration between 1956 and 1977. This provided a way of using IQ data and other attributes to predict health-related behaviors in later adulthood. When they looked at type of alcoholic beverage preferred, they found a 30-point higher IQ in wine drinkers over those who drank primarily beer or spirits. In fact, a sort of dose-response relationship emerged; the stronger the preference for wine, the higher the baseline IQ. Interestingly, there was no relationship between intelligence and alcoholism, which bolsters the view that it has a genetic basis.

What this type of study can't tell us is whether drinking wine makes one smart, only that smart people drink wine. But given the evidence that wine polyphenols activate enzymes involved in learning and memory centers of the brain, it seems like a self-reinforcing process. Either way, it is certainly food– or drink–for thought.

The difficulties in making determinations such as the potential benefits of anticoagulants on neurological decline could be partly overcome with population studies. Despite the appealingly plausible theory of an important role for anticoagulants in this regard, though, the supporting data is sparse. Population studies comparing wine consumption to Alzheimer's disease and other manifestations of neurological deterioration, on the other hand, are compelling and the data is dramatic, as we shall see. Clearly there is something else about wine and the brain, and once again it is the polyphenols that are in the spotlight.

Both acute and long-term benefits are seen with the wine studies. Gradual cognitive decline, whether from Alzheimer's disease or progressively impaired microcirculation is of central concern for anti-aging, but acute stroke is a life-threatening event. Survivors of stroke are often severely impaired, because brain cells are so vulnerable to loss of blood flow (ischemia) for even brief periods. Any advantage here can make an important difference.

A research team from the University of Missouri found intriguing evidence that resveratrol can significantly attenuate nerve cell damage from stroke. They employed an experimental model using gerbils, in whom a stroke was induced by occluding the arteries supplying the brain for five minutes. They then compared three groups: no treatment, administration of resveratrol during occlusion (meaning it only got to the brain after blood flow was restored), and pre-treatment with reveratrol. Both of the resveratrol-treated groups fared dramatically better that the non-treatment control group.* These findings jive with other reports of wine phenolics and ischemia-reperfusion injury in other organs.

Was there something unique about resveratrol, or is it simply an antioxidant effect that protects the brain during stroke? A 2003 study from the Johns Hopkins University identified an additional possibility. They looked more closely at what happens to brain cells during the period of oxygen starvation. Among the many insults that the tissue sustains, an important one is direct oxidative damage mediated by a fickle molecule called heme (Chapter 2). This is the iron-based oxygen carrier in blood cells, and found in red meat (it is in fact what makes it red.)

---

* They further demonstrated that resveratrol enters the brain tissue, an important finding since many biomolecules are unable to cross what is known as the "blood-brain barrier."

When oxygen is lacking, heme accumulates and may turn against its host, fomenting a riot of free radicals. Antioxidants are helpful in countering the uprising, but an enzyme called *heme oxygenase* is best equipped for the job. Resveratrol appears to stimulate heme oxygenase production and activity, thereby reinforcing its antioxidant effects.

Oxidative stress and the brain

Brain cells suffer from oxidative stress over the long term also, probably more than any other tissue. So while it may be logical to presume that there would be some advantage afforded by red wine (based on what we now know), attention has historically been directed at antioxidant vitamins. The role of dietary antioxidants and degenerative brain disease is a difficult one to ascertain, however, because cognitive impairment itself leads to poor nutritional habits, and so it is earlier lifelong nutrition that needs to be assessed. Antioxidant diets (e.g., the Mediterranean) tend to include red wine anyway.

The question of whether vitamin supplements can reduce the risk of age-related cognitive disorders remained an open one for quite some time. There have in fact been quite a few studies attempting to address this issue, typically involving vitamins C and/or E. A meta-analysis of these trials found meager evidence of effectiveness, though there are a few suggesting that combination therapy with both C and E might be helpful. However, daily supplementation with more than 400 units of vitamin E has also been associated with an *increased* risk of premature all-cause death, and excessive doses of C aren't risk-free either. Given these findings, and the fact that wine polyphenols are so much more effective as antioxidants, it is difficult to assign a major role to vitamins in an antioxidant strategy for Alzheimer's.

Alcohol probably does make a contribution, on the other hand, by virtue of its ability to prevent vascular disease (by improving the cholesterol profile and prevention of clots) but these effects are at least partly offset by its toxicity to brain cells. Alcohol has in fact been directly implicated in neurodegenerative conditions (such as Wernicke's

Wine for Memory

Gutenberg is acknowledged as the inventor of movable type in the mid-fifteenth century, and every schoolchild learns that the first book to be reproduced in quantity was the Bible. But it wasn't much later that the earliest book on wine, a tome known as *De Vinis,* was printed. It was based on the earlier writings of one Arnaldo da Villanova (1235-1311), described as a physician, surgeon, botanist, alchemist and philosopher, who was a prolific writer and an expert on wine and its healing properties. He was widely traveled and renowned in his time, having made house calls on Pope Clement V in Avignon, the King of Aragon James II, Frederick III of Sicily, and many others.

His prescriptions provide a fascinating insight into medieval medicine. A rosemary-infused wine whose recipe he attributed to Galen "strengthens by its own virtue the substance of the heart and thus keeps people young" and suggested that "perhaps the body of those who use it permanently will not decay". But my favorite is his "wine that brings back the memory and which is good for forgetfulness" which is made by steeping ginger, peppers, cloves and other spices into "good fermenting wine". He recommends it also for "warming cold people and for drying moist people" and notes that it "helps also against all flatulence of evil moisture". Something to keep in mind.

encephalopathy, basically the brain pickled in alcohol, and peripheral neuropathy, a deterioration of the nerves in the extremities) at least in high doses. Can wine phenolics work in isolation to prevent Alzheimer's disease? The relevant question here is what the net effect is, with moderate wine drinking habits, over the long term.

Nevertheless, the supposition that wine could contribute to *improved* mental function, particularly with advancing age, seems so intuitively untenable that no one bothered to look until the French paradox report

---

A quercetin curiosity

Resveratrol may have taken the early lead as the primary brain boosting polyphenol, but researchers from the Institute of Biological Medical Electronic Engineering from the University of Nanjing in China weighed in with a 2006 report looking at quercetin on spatial learning and memory in mice. The classic test of ability to negotiate through a maze, and to remember the route for subsequent forays, was improved with quercetin supplementation. The results were attributed to enhanced brain enzyme activity in the cerebral cortex as well as a memory center known as the hippocampus. This of course implies bioavailability of orally ingested wine phenolics in brain tissue, though much remains to be learned about the precise nature of this intriguing interaction.

---

broke the mold. Standard medical advice had always been to discourage geriatric drinking, given the reduced ability to metabolize alcohol that accompanies aging. Once again, researchers knew that they had to take extra care to ensure that their research protocols surpassed the highest standards in order for their findings to have a chance of being published. And again it was a French connection that delivered the goods.

Debunking assumptions

It was one of Serge Renaud's colleagues, Dr. Jean-Marc Orgogozo who took the lead in examining the established assumptions about wine and age-related mental function. Dr. Orgogozo, a neuropsychologist and chairman of the Department of Neurology at the University Hospital Pellegrin in Bordeaux, began a study in 1988 to test the potential association between wine and cognitive impairment. The researchers enrolled 3,777 residents age 65 or older from dozens of towns and villages around Bordeaux. The baseline data observed that about 60%

drank regularly, with 95% of those drinking mostly red wine.* The results were published in France in 1997 and later in the American Journal of Epidemiology. Incredibly, *senile dementia and Alzheimer's were found to be 75-80% less prevalent in moderate wine drinkers as compared to nondrinkers* at the beginning of the study. As the study population matured, the difference diminished, but after eight years moderate red wine drinkers still held a 50% edge over their teetotaling cohorts.

Imagine if a drug with similar efficacy were introduced. Even if the percentages were substantially smaller, it would no doubt be a blockbuster success. In fact, if it only helped 10% of subjects delay the onset of senility, that would translate into some 400,000 seniors benefited. Given the expected increase in senile dementia cases, this same 10% multiplies into millions. If the figure is indeed closer to 80%, it could be one of the most significant public health developments ever. But again we are reminded that wine polyphenols have not been tested as a drug; what we do know is that wine drinkers appear much less likely to become senile.

With findings as dramatic as these, it is reasonable to demand independent confirmation. After all, the scientific method on which we rely requires it. Simply having a plausible explanation and one epidemiological study joins only two parts of a larger puzzle; we need to see if the observational data holds up and then look into the biochemical reasons for it.

Confirmation came immediately from the Framingham study, in a report also published in The American Journal of Epidemiology. Their motivation, however, may have been different; these authors recognized that earlier studies had in fact shown alcohol to be associated with poorer mental function, as most would assume. But when subsequent studies looking more closely at the moderate wine consumer subset began to reverse the prevailing view, it appeared that only women were the beneficiaries of the vine. In contrast to the French study, men did not appear to get the same benefit as women in terms of cognitive measures, at least in the early studies. Studies of this type tend to be small, though, and so the large study group available to the Framingham researchers provided an opportunity to address the question more definitively.

---

*   Their definitions of moderate drinking were generous: two to three 4.5-oz. glasses daily for women, three to four for men!

This research group was a collaboration between the Department of Neurology at the Boston University School of Medicine, the Department of Psychology at the University of Maine, and others affiliated with the Framingham project. The study subject group consisted of approximately 1800 men and women between ages 55 and 88. After compiling data about alcohol consumption habits, and potential confounding variables, the subjects were given a series of neuropsychological tests known as the Kaplan-Albert battery. This includes measures of overall cognitive performance as well as short-term and long-term memory.

> *Wine, a friend of the body and of the mind, predisposes men to all mental work. We should all be remorseless lovers of wine and its faithful defenders.*
> —Professor Portman, member of l'Academie de Medicine

(Qouted in *The Vade Mecum of the Wine Lover*, Andre Mournetas and Henry Pelissier, 1951; translated by William Buckley and Claude Landry)

Although women at a moderate level of drinking still did better overall than men, superior performance in several areas was observed in both genders. Part of the difference was thought to be attributable to a higher incidence of high blood pressure and diabetes in men. Nevertheless, the finding that moderate drinking helps prevent age-related cognitive decline was confirmed.

A report from Italy in 2001 provided further momentum. This project, a combined effort between the Catholic University of Rome, Wake Forest University in North Carolina, and Brown University in Rhode Island evaluated some 15,800 hospitalized older patients. This group of Italian subjects consumed red wine as their primary alcohol source. Overall, abstainers were found to have a 29% incidence of cognitive impairment, with drinkers having a 19% incidence. When adjusted for confounding variables and plotted against average daily consumption, the familiar J-shaped curve emerged. Incredibly, even drinkers of up to a liter of wine daily performed better than nondrinkers! As would be expected, women required a lower intake (less than a half-liter) and as one would guess they tested poorly at levels of a liter a day, an intake certainly well above the diagnostic threshold for alcoholism. Keep in mind that these parameters describe lifelong drinking habits, so the tests reflect cumulative changes rather than acute effects.

Major Studies on Wine and Alzheimer's

Canadian Study of Health and Aging (2002, American Journal of Epidemiology) *Cohort study examining 6,434 subjects. Wine, coffee, non-steroidal anti-inflammatories (e.g., ibuprofen) and regular exercise associated with lower risk.*

Copenhagen City Heart Study (2002, American Academy of Neurology) *Case-control study within a cohort of 1709 subjects age 65 and older enrolled 15 years earlier. Wine consumption but not beer or spirits correlated with lower risk.*

Catholic University of Rome multicenter survey (Alcoholism, Clinical and Experimental Research, 2001) *Population study of 15,807 subjects. Lower risk of dementia in wine drinkers up to 1 liter/day for men, 0.5 liters/day for women.*

Bordeaux Study (European Journal of Epidemiology, 2000) *Cohort study of 3,777 subjects age 65 and older. Risk of dementia 80% lower in wine drinkers as compared to nondrinkers.*

As they had done earlier with heart disease, Mørten Gronbaek and colleagues provided the final keystone. A widely reported study published in November of 2002 provided data from a 15-year cohort study found that wine, but not beer or spirits, was associated with a substantially lower risk of dementia. The concept that wine helps the brain began to register with some.

With the epidemiologic data accumulating, the focus shifts to the laboratory to identify a cause-and-effect explanation. Given the known role of oxidative stress in aging of a variety of tissues, and our developing understanding of how wine polyphenols protect the brain during stroke, wine-derived phenolic antioxidants seem a logical place to start. Several lines of research implicate oxidative stress as a primary cause of nerve cell death associated with Alzheimer's, Parkinson's, and senility. Free radicals attack DNA as well as critical proteins and other vital biochemicals indiscriminately. All of this eventually culminates in cell death and degenerative neurological disease.

A plan for the apes: calorie restriction

The Gerontology Research Center at the National Institute of Aging, National Institutes of Health, has been putting their primates on a diet. Specifically, they have been looking at the effects of caloric restriction on aging in a number of ways, including brain health. (If you're concerned about mistreatment of these simian subjects, remember that this isn't anything that humans aren't doing voluntarily.) The overriding question here has to do with lifespan extension, but some important findings about mental function are emerging as well.

Both long-term and shorter (6 month) restriction by 30% appears to retard the onset of age-related declines in several specific parameters in rhesus monkeys, whose aging closely resembles that of humans. These include fine muscle coordination as well as overall muscle action, what researchers call "locomotor" activity. Current work is evaluating the possible effects on the part of the brain associated with Parkinson's disease, and "neuroprotection" against such things as oxidative stress or stroke. It remains to be determined whether sirtuins are the agents of caloric restriction in the brain, and whether or not wine phenolics can produce the same benefits, but given the overall picture it seems likely.

Protective details

It is difficult, if not impossible, to directly measure the effects of wine or other dietary interventions on the living brain. Nerve cells can be grown in a

What is the difference between Alzheimer's disease and senile dementia?

Both senile dementia and Alzheimer's are forms of mental deterioration associated with aging, so it can be difficult to tell the difference. Alzheimer's is characterized by gradual death of brain cells, believed to be related to deposits of protein called *amyloid*. About 60-70% of senile dementia cases are due to Alzheimer's disease.

Typical signs of Alzheimer's include:

— memory loss
— problems doing familiar tasks
— problems with language
— problems knowing date, time, or place
— poor or decreased judgment
— problems with abstract thinking
— changes in mood or behavior
— changes in personality

A thorough medical evaluation is necessary to confirm a diagnosis of Alzheimer's disease, and alcohol in any form is to be avoided in established cases of senile dementia of any type. Unfortunately, wine polyphenols may not be able to reverse the course of senile dementia once it has been diagnosed, but a lifetime pattern of moderate consumption appears to substantially reduce the risk.

culture, however, where they can be subjected to a variety of insults and tested against potentially protective agents. One study from London, published in 2000, evaluated the ability of wine polyphenols to protect cultured nerve cells from damage from oxidized LDL cholesterol (abbreviated oxLDL), which is as damaging to nerve tissue as to arterial lining.

Unsheltered nerve cells exposed to oxLDL experience DNA fragmentation and eventual cell death. As we have come to expect, flavonoids and other polyphenols exerted marked protective effects in this experiment. Importantly, the researchers also found evidence that specific structural aspects of the polyphenols' molecular makeup that seemed to be responsible. In other words, the effect was not due simply to a nonspecific antioxidant effect alone. Wine-specific polyphenols appear to have yet another unique role in protecting brain cells.

Our familiar nemesis COX-2 turns out to have a role in Alzheimer's disease as well. A research group in the Netherlands found elevated levels of COX-2 in the specific populations of nerve cells whose deterioration causes Alzheimer's. Since we know that wine polyphenols inhibit COX-2 activity, this provides yet another potential explanation for the protective effect of wine against mental decline. The finding in the Canadian study that anti-inflammatory medication use (also COX enzyme antagonists) correlates to lower risk reinforces the concept of chronic inflammation as an underlying causative mechanism.

The final piece of evidence

Oxidative damage, COX-2 hyperactivity and impaired blood circulation to the brain may provide plausible explanations for generalized cognitive decline with age, but Alzheimer's is a particularly onerous beast and not fully explained by these factors alone. One important clue is the deposition of proteins called *amyloid* in the brain. While we know that accumulation of crosslinked proteins is generally associated with aging, the amyloid plaques in the brain have a significant association with Alzheimer's. A group of scientists at the Scripps Research Institute in California proposed that chronic inflammation and amyloid interact in a way that makes the amyloid protein molecules "misfold." It is this specific abnormality that causes them to aggregate and invade nerve cells. Regardless of the precise mechanism, it is becoming clear that amyloid plays a key role in the pathogenesis of Alzheimer's.

This is where the most solid connection is found between low risk of Alzheimer's disease and red wine. Separate research teams from Italy and Japan reported in 2003 that red wine polyphenols help to break down these amyloid deposits. They counteract the toxicity of amyloid to the nerve cell as well as helping to prevent the formation of amyloid plaques. The observations show a clear "dose-response" relationship and are not explained by an antioxidant effect alone; in other words, there is some specific interaction that occurs at a molecular level between polyphenols and amyloid proteins. A conformational study from the Mount Sinai School of Medicine in New York, published in 2007, demonstrated that mice prone to Alzheimer's experienced significantly less deterioration of spatial memory function when cabernet sauvignon was included in their diet. They were able to link this to a reduction in beta-amyloid through an effect on processing a precursor protein. (The effect was not found when they were given alcohol in similar amounts or water only.) Although much remains to be learned about the role of amyloid in the genesis of Alzheimer's disease, the data supports the epidemiologic findings and fit the overall picture neatly.

Wine is the glass of the mind.

—Erasmus

We should observe that the protective effect of wine phenolics against Alzheimer's is seen with the whole class of compounds, including tannins, but the focus has shifted to resveratrol. (One study found that catechin, a wine flavonoid, was actually more effective than resveratrol at protecting nerve cells from amyloid toxicity.) Early data from studies of Huntington's disease—another brain disorder related to nerve cell degeneration—revealed that reveratrol might be therapeutic in a unique way, by modulating gene expression (signal transduction) for sirtuins. These are of course the same enzymes involved in the caloric restriction-longevity effect, here playing a role in neuronal protection. Other pathways are being uncovered as well.

A satisfactory explanation of wine's ability to prevent Alzheimer's disease, then, involves polyphenols policing aberrant amyloid molecules. But what causes their delinquency in the first place? Another report from Scripps details a process of chronic inflammation, leading to oxidative damage as an important spark. This would integrate well with the theory of oxidation as an underlying mechanism of aging, and explain why

NSAID's (anti-inflammatories) appear to have some benefit.* Oxidative stress and inflammation are also known to be risk factors for Parkinson's disease, another condition associated with a neurotoxic protein, in this case one called *alpha-synuclein.* In both Alzheimer's and Parkinson's, oxidation products are found in the brains of affected individuals. Because wine phenolics are such obsessive antioxidants, they are in a position to provide upstream protection against the cascade of reactions that are causative for a number of degenerative brain conditions.

Since Alzheimer's is characterized by gradual death of brain cells, we might expect that any alcoholic beverage will hasten the progress of the disease. We are reminded that alcohol can indeed be a *cause* of dementia, even at a younger age. As far as we know, the role of wine in senile dementia is one of prevention, not treatment. That is one reason why it is so important to establish a pattern of healthful drinking at an early age. Fortunately, effective medical therapies are being developed for Alzheimer's, and the earlier the disease is diagnosed and treatment started, the better. Notably, these drugs generally aim to boost the function of faltering brain cells, rather than attack the underlying causes.

MAP of the brain

While most researchers were focusing on the epidemiology of wine and senile dementia, a group at the University of Milan was looking at direct effects of wine polyphenols on nerve cell function. In order for nerve cells to communicate with each other, an enzyme called *mitogen activated protein,* or MAP, is required. This process is fundamental to memory, learning, and for that matter all aspects of higher mental function. Active learning processes are associated with higher levels of activated MAP in specific areas of the brain.

---

* Because of evidence that NSAID's might lower the risk of Alzheimer's, prospective trials have been conducted but these were discontinued due to side-effects of using these medications for extended periods of time, just as the COX-2 inhibitor trials for cancer prevention were halted when cardiac complications appeared.

The dope on wine

Here's where the story on wine and the brain takes a "through the looking glass" turn. Cell surface receptors for resveratrol and other wine polyphenols have been identified in brain tissue, and are felt to be responsible for many of the antioxidant and other protective effects. Although the receptor molecule has not been isolated, enough is known to recognize certain similarities to cannabinoid receptors, according to scientists at the University of Arkansas. These are of course the very molecules that respond to *Cannabis satvia,* or marijuana. Even more interesting is that *Cannabis* seems to have some antioxidant activity. But resveratrol doesn't produce the psychoactive effects of marijuana, so there is more to the story.

In order to clear the air and see what's really going on, the researchers studied the interactions between resveratrol and the turmeric compound curcumin (Chapter 7) and cannabinoid receptors in brain tissue. The methodology is fairly arcane stuff, but the upshot is that there was binding of both resveratrol and curcumin to the receptors in a way that competed with *Cannabis*. Complicating it further is the fact that there are different *Cannabis* receptors mediating different effects, such as inflammation and pain, hunger cravings, and addiction behaviors. The goal of this research is to find a compound that produces desirable effects in terms of analgesia and other properties of *Cannabis* without certain responses that some would consider undesirable. To date, no such substance has been found. What the resveratrol and curcumin receptor binding patterns reveal is a suggestion of what such a molecule might look like. It may also explain why wine drinkers are less likely to have problems with weight. Not that a glass of great Bordeaux hasn't ever brought to mind a good steak. With a truffle demi-glace.

In a human nerve cell culture, the investigators exposed the tissue to resveratrol, one of the better known wine polyphenols. Significant increases in levels of activated MAP were found with the addition of resveratrol in amounts equivalent to moderate wine drinking. This would help nerve cells in the brain communicate with each other more easily, translating directly to improved memory and cognition. So wine polyphenols not only protect the brain from oxidative stress and the resultant degenerative conditions, they might actually make you smarter.

Though this one small step toward understanding how wine enhances brain function is significant, it is a giant leap of logic to assume that it explains everything. It seems highly unlikely that this acute effect explains the overall reduction in dementia risk. The accrued benefits of a lifetime of daily antioxidant protection cannot be made up for in a crash course. Oxidative stress is a continuous onslaught that begins with our first breath, so its effects are cumulative. But it is reassuring to know that it is never too late to start reaping the benefits of a red wine-based anti-aging strategy.

How wine protects the brain

Breakdown of amyloid prevents Alzheimer's

COX-2 inhibition protects nerve cells

Increased MAP enzyme activity enhances nerve cell interaction

Decreased vascular disease preserves blood supply

Protection from oxidative stress

Those who do not or should not have alcohol can still benefit from the research. Dr. Orgogozo looked at not just wine, but diets high in other sources of polyphenols. Although not as bountiful a source as wine, vegetable-rich diets appear to be associated with measurable reductions in senility as well.

There is of course more to the picture than wine and other dietary sources of polyphenols. It is interesting to note however that all of the identified biochemical risk factors for Alzheimer's disease—amyloid, oxidative damage, cardiovascular disease, and up-regulation of COX-2—are counteracted by wine polyphenols. Other factors associated with longevity in general have also been shown to lower the odds. These include things such as regular exercise and staying mentally active. It is now known that brain cells are able to regenerate, despite early assumptions to the contrary. Exercising the mind by cultivating curiosity helps keep it fit and better able to withstand some inevitable loss of function with age. Challenging one's assumptions is an excellent form of mental exercise, and the topic of wine and the brain certainly provides an opportunity for some to do just that.

No one can say for sure that intangible factors such an abiding sense of humor and a positive outlook can alter the risk of senility. But these do seem do be associated with extreme longevity, and few sufferers of dementia survive for a great many years beyond the diagnosis. It seems self-evident that those with a lifelong tendency toward moderation, enjoyment of life, and good wine and food also generally have active minds and that this would translate into tangible health benefits. It has been said that an idle mind is the Devil's workshop, but as Benjamin Franklin wrote, "wine is proof that God loves us and wants us to be happy." Hold that thought.

> *"Well kept, it always improves as it approaches its eighth or tenth year; it is then a balm for the elderly, the feeble and the disabled, and will restore life to the dying."*
> —from a 1794 auction catalogue for the vineyard Romanée-Conti

Chapter 10

Wine is a Food

Wine . . . is a food.

—Oliver Wendell Holmes,
in a letter to the Massachusetts Medical Society

Pill Talk

Many of us who grew up in the 1950's and '60's remember the utopian visions of a technological future. "Better living through chemistry" was the motto of Monsanto's Tomorrowland exhibit at Disneyland. All-electric kitchens, sleek cars with fins evocative of B-movie sci-fi spaceships, and preprocessed meals available at the touch of a button would whisk us through the day. In fact, meals *per se* would be unnecessary, as all of our nutritional needs could be put into a pill. The nuisance of wasting valuable time for eating would no longer slow us down.

Ironically, a Flintstone's type diet may have been healthier than futuristic Jetson's engineered cuisine. The prototypical Stone Age human diet likely favored berries, greens, and vegetables more than meat, and most certainly not boat-sized portions of dinosaur ribs. Since we also have evidence that as soon as early humans discovered ways to contain and store liquids, the particular aspects of fermented grape juice came to be appreciated, and so wine with supper is a tradition probably as old as civilization. Cro-magnon connoisseurs may not have fawned over the subtleties of merlot with mastodon or gamay Beaujolais with grilled wild game, but the marriage of food and wine was sealed from the beginning.

Plato's plate

So we see that the concept of wine in moderation as an essential element of a healthful diet is an ancient one. The 4th-5th century BC Greek philosopher Plato wrote expansively on wine and diet, considering the gods' gift to humans "a medicine given for the purpose of securing modesty of soul and health and strength of body." Interestingly, he also associated moderation of nourishment with longevity, presaging modern science by two and a half millennia. (He does not appear to have advocated the extreme practice of caloric restriction however.)

The view of wine as a medicine did not imply that it wasn't a food, but rather the opposite; the practice of medicine was defined by Plato as "the art that renders to bodies drugs, foods, and drinks." Diet was considered a scientific discipline and a central aspect of medical care. If wine was medicine, then foods were drugs, one being equally likely as the other to be prescribed for ailments. Moderation and balance ware the guiding principles, a concept considered quaint in modern culture.

For most though, simply finding enough to eat remained a primary concern as it does throughout so much of the world today; survival until the next week took priority over shooting for centenarian status. So the next major attempt at recording traditions and wisdom about diet and health didn't appear for quite some time. A Latin tome known as the *Regimen Sanitatis Salernitani* from the eleventh century advised about wine: "During meals drink wine happily, little but often" and "To avoid harming the body never drink between meals." *The Book of Wine,* apparently compiled in the early fourteenth century and printed in 1478, and attributed to the medical writer and court physician to James II of Aragon, Arnoldo da Villanova (1253-1315) noted that wine "fortifies the brain and the natural strength ... causes foods to be digested and produces good blood." These treatises represented the soundest reasoning of their day, integrating nutritional and philosophical considerations. It would not be until the second half of the twentieth century that the scientific basis for considering wine as a food would be demonstrated. Paradoxically, these ancient practices of healthful eating and drinking were simultaneously diverging even further from contemporary trends even as growing scientific validation of their importance began to come to light.

Diets and doctors

Inventing a weight loss diet is surely the shortest path to publishing success for a physician, but the tradition of doctors advising on nutrition is an ancient one. In fact, well up to and beyond the Renaissance, dietary counseling was a central part of any successful medical practice. (It may have been one of the few useful things medieval physicians did.) An important medical text of 1547 called the *Breviary of Health* observed that "A good cook is half a physician." A close collaboration between chefs and doctors was the norm, perhaps a notion worth reviving. Maybe I should have called this book *The Wine Diet*. Wine drinkers are, after all, statistically much less likely to be overweight. To what degree this attributes to the biochemistry of wine or to the fact that wine informs a meal with a more leisurely and sensible manner may not be measurable, but the result is an alchemy for healthy living that medieval practitioners may have understood better than many of their modern counterparts.

The lifestyle habits espoused by Plato are the foundation of what eventually came to be known as the Mediterranean diet, though interest in it isn't a particularly new phenomenon, even if the science behind it is. In the 1950's, a now-classic book called *Seven Countries* was published by Professor Ancel Keys of the University of Minnesota. The book was the result of a study comparing cardiovascular disease and longevity between developed and less-developed countries. Surprisingly (at least to many at the time) the residents of the Greek island of Crete were found to enjoy the longest life expectancy despite poor access to health care services, and their mortality rate from cardiovascular disease was only 10% of that in the United States. Wine consumption with meals was one of the defining facets of the lifestyle. Interestingly, they were also noted to be heavy smokers and have a relatively high fat intake, a Cretan Conundrum presaging what would later be called the French Paradox. We physicians should take note of just how healthy these wine-drinking but doctor-deprived people were compared to those who could more readily avail themselves of our advice.

The Traditional Healthy Mediterranean Diet Pyramid

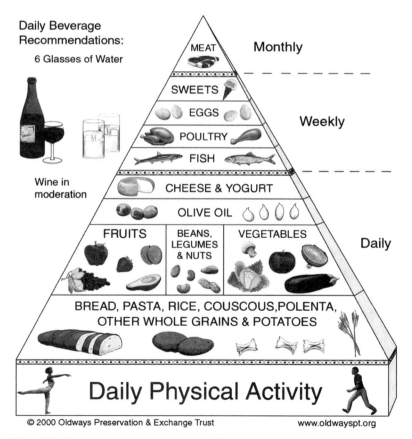

The Mediterranean Diet Pyramid, reproduced with permission from Oldways Preservation Trust

Paradigm for a New Pyramid

The observations about longevity and diet in the Mediterranean went largely unnoticed for at least thirty years. Perhaps the developed countries were preoccupied with the Cold War and related disaster planning, or simply unwilling to seriously consider the possibility that a lifestyle based upon a relatively high calorie intake, largely from fats, could be healthy. There was certainly some conflict with emerging findings about smoking, cholesterol, and heart disease, and most were not ready to open-mindedly investigate the issue of wine as a plus for health. Eventually, professor Walter Willet of the Department of Nutrition at the Harvard School of Public Health came across the data, and in 1993 he published a revised version of the "food pyramid" based upon the Mediterranean concept. A version of this can be seen on the U.S. Department of Agriculture website, with a glass of red wine at the flank.

Bonhomie in a Bottle

Healthy eating involves more than nutritional chemistry; *how* you eat may be as important as *what* you eat. The same is true for wine. Epidemiologic studies tell us that it is not only the amount, but the pattern of drinking that is critical for healthful advantage. We know, for example, that binge drinkers fare poorly by comparison to regular drinkers even if their overall intake of alcohol is moderate. The J-shaped curve applies only to regular, moderate drinking, just as there is little benefit to only eating vegetables on weekends.

It is also true that people who drink wine, especially those who have a glass or two with dinner, tend to have healthier lifestyles in several other ways, at least in northern Europe and North America. The Mediterranean diet is more correctly considered a lifestyle, a way of living more than a compilation of food intake patterns. The subjects on Crete, and Jeanne Calment's *Provençeaux* cohorts led active, rustic, outdoor lives for the most part. Wine with lunch was not unusual (and thankfully the most dangerous vehicle employed in the afternoon was most likely a tractor or a bicycle.) Though these linked behaviors are increasingly at odds with modern urban life, they cannot be dismissed.

Is wine on your grocery list?

One of the dilemmas researchers face in trying to interpret patterns of human behaviors is in trying to determine in which direction the cause→effect arrow points. What the data provides is associations. For example, people who have low rates of a specific degenerative disease may not only be more likely to drink wine, but they typically tend have other healthy dietary habits; but how much is related to the wine and how much to eating their vegetables?

It is possible to gain some insight into this by analyzing grocery buying patterns, which is actually not all that difficult because supermarket chains already collect massive amounts of data for purposes of market analysis. The data can be aggregated so as to determine what products tend to be purchased in the same transaction with other products. They do this sort of thing all the time, but some of the data is also useful to health researchers.

With the permission of two supermarket chains in Denmark, Morten Grønbaek's team looked at what wine and beer buyers tended to include in their shopping carts by analyzing some 3.5 million transactions. (Liquor is not sold in grocery stores there, so they were not able to look at what spirits drinkers eat.) As one might expect, wine buyers bought more olives, fruit, vegetables, low-fat cheese, poultry, and meat, while beer drinkers went for the ready-cooked meals, sugar, cold cuts, chips, sausages, and soft drinks. My interpretation of this is that wine seems to be considered to be more like a food, part of a meal, while beer resides more in the context of snacking. So wine consumption is, in part at least, a statistical marker for other healthy habits, and a sensible diet tends to include wine. In this case, the arrow points both ways.

These various lifestyle pattern elements can of course be accounted for mathematically; they are among the aforementioned "confounding variables" that can blur the interpretation of studies. While we can with assurance distill out the independent contributions of wine, there is no doubting the importance of *frequency* in addition to moderation. Regular wine drinkers tend to have healthier diets and exercise more, even if the French still smoke like—well, the French.* In general, wine drinkers eat more vegetables and fish. As a group they are better educated, which may explain in part wine's "snob appeal."

More specifically, it is not only the pattern of drinking moderate amounts on a regular basis, but actually having wine with meals that

---

Eyes on the Price

Perfectly drinkable and enjoyable wines are available at a variety of price points, and some frankly average wines are sold at astronomical markups based on past reputation or rarity. But if wine is to become a regular at the dinner table, for most of us the cost is an important consideration. Does it make a difference as far as health is concerned?

In order to answer this, we need to consider the fact that grapevines make the beneficial polyphenols when they are stressed. Too much stress and the grapes might just give up, too little and they will not make interesting and flavorful wines. Boosting the phenolics usually means reducing yields and paying very close attention to the vineyard, a time-consuming and labor-intensive process. So for the most part your $10 bottle doesn't pack the vitamin W punch as much as one costing $25 or more. Perhaps it's a matter of balancing one's financial health against physical and mental well-being! Just don't raid your retirement plan, you may need it to last a long time.

---

* Since the first edition France has actually banned indoor smoking. Though there is widespread lamentation about the loss of their café culture, one can only hope that they continue to practice healthy wine drinking.

is important. It's more than slowing down the absorption of alcohol; there are physiologic reasons for it. And while it can't be scientifically measured, at least part of the answer is simply slowing down and enjoying the pleasures of the table with family and friends. If you think of wine as a food, it becomes one of the few pleasures that the "diet police" can't cite you for as long as you obey the speed limit. Red wine *is* in fact a food, not only nutritious in unique ways but also one that most embodies the simple celebrations of everyday life.

> *Wine makes daily living easier, less hurried, with fewer tensions and more tolerance.*
>
> —Benjamin Franklin

Many foods, like wine, have a silently sinister side-effect when taken improperly. Recall how James Bond's *M* advised against too much red meat and white bread in order to counteract the free radicals? These and many other foods dump loads of oxidized fats and carbohydrates into the blood stream, leading in turn to an onslaught of free radicals. This phenomenon can be measured and is termed "postprandial oxidative stress." So while calories and saturated fats (not to mention trans fats) may be important for controlling cholesterol levels and weight gain, it is the oxidative damage from food that accelerates aging.

There are several ways to assess postprandial oxidative stress. One relatively simple method is to look at the cholesterol lipoproteins, in particular LDL. Remember that it is the oxidized version that is most active in formation of plaques in arteries and generalized tissue damage, including brain cells. Wine taken with meals has been shown to minimize the postprandial rise in oxidized LDL, and all but abolish the "oxidizability" of already circulating lipoproteins. This has been measured in both humans and animal studies, and has been shown to be related to the polyphenols. The effect is present at moderate levels of wine consumption as long as it is ingested with the meal.

Food is a Drug

It might be argued that any alcoholic beverage, even one containing a bounty of healthful flavonoids, must be a drug because of the distinct potential for intoxication. This assumes that the purpose of drinking wine is inebriation. It should also be pointed out that

---

Are you allergic to wine?

If you are one of the many people who have experienced an allergic type reaction to wine, you have probably experienced the frustration of trying to figure out which wines cause the reaction and which ones are ok. Perhaps you had a wine in Europe that you enjoyed but the same or similar wine back home caused a problem, or a wine you have always loved one day gives you a headache. Often the sulfites added to most wines are blamed, but these occur naturally in wine in small amounts, and true sulfite allergies aren't all that common. Although labels on wine bottles in the U.S. are required to advise "contains sulfites" if the amount is greater than 10 parts per million, this is below the threshold of the amounts that occur naturally. But it probably isn't additives, the type of oak used for the aging barrels, or the grape variety that is the culprit. As it turns out, certain bacterial contaminants in wine produce histamine, the chemical mediator of so many of the symptoms of an allergy attack; so it usually isn't a true allergy, it just feels like one. (Histamine is only one of a family of nasty molecules called *biogenic amines* which may appear inconspicuously but regularly in red wine.) The bacteria don't announce their presence through any sensory means, and they tend to show up randomly. The taste and smell of the wine is unaffected. The good news is that a relatively simple test that can detect the histamine, though it isn't exactly suited for home use. Best bet is to take an antihistamine and try something else for a while.

foods can have profound effects on the body and mind as well. For example, contemporary thinking about diet emphasizes the importance of limiting or balancing carbohydrate intake (carbohydrates are most readily converted to sugar in the blood stream.) That is because white bread and other processed carbohydrates have what is called a high *glycemic index,* which means that blood sugar levels are elevated rapidly; this is followed by a burst of insulin release that precipitously brings blood sugar back down, often overshooting the target level. For some, this means merely feeling sleepy an hour or so after a meal, but for many it can mean near-somnolence.

Other food components such as the amino acid *tryptophan* (think Thanksgiving turkey) are known to be readily metabolized into soporific substances. And the simple *volume* of food of any type can lead to diversion of blood flow to the gastrointestinal tract for digestion and enlistment of nutrients. All of this results in depressed brain function, which can be as profound as the effects of alcohol. And any doubt about the possibility for abuse of food, and its potential for addiction, is readily countered by the burgeoning epidemic of obesity[*]. If food isn't a drug, it certainly acts like one sometimes; so the distinction between wine and other foods is more arbitrary that it might seem at first blush.

Slow Food, Fast Friends

We are a fast food society. The notion of a family dinner seems like a quaint old-world holdover to many, out of phase with the realities of modern life. Wine as a normal, everyday part of a meal was never reintegrated into the American lifestyle after prohibition, and has gradually been fading from modern Europe as well. Culinary trends from the 1940's on were more focused on processed foods, storage, and convenience of preparation than on wholesomeness. Even the burger joints of the 1950's eventually ceased to be gathering places where family and friends could linger over a meal, as drive-in was replaced by drive-through.

---

[*] Approximately 2/3 of Americans are overweight, and more than 20% are considered morbidly obese. Obesity-related illnesses and premature deaths are vastly greater than those that are alcohol-related.

(A professor at the Culinary Institute of America recently calculated that nearly 1 in 5 meals are eaten in cars, usually while driving.)

And healthy drinking patterns? Many counties throughout the U.S. remained "dry" well into the latter part of the twentieth century. Decent everyday wine became an American anachronism, and even Great Britain suffered what Evelyn Waugh called the "barbarous divorce of fermented liquor from food" in the post-war years.* This trend away from social to solitary eating is mirrored in drinking patterns as well, which has been shown to have specific health consequences. A study published in 2009 from Japan, with data from 19,000 subjects followed prospectively for an average of 10 years, found a lowered incidence of stroke in social drinkers as opposed to solitary drinkers, at least in the moderate drinking cohort.

There were efforts to reverse these trends though, notably by maverick culinary guru Julia Child. Her cooking show of the 1960's, a revolutionary concept in itself, were even more remarkable for their attempt to get Americans to think about cooking French. And not just French cuisine, but a healthy measure of wine in the cook as well as on the table. Her vitality well into her 90's is a testament to the *joie de vivre* of a lifestyle centered on the indulgences of the table.

How do we get out of the fast food lane and onto the scenic route? Those who rebel against the fast paced aspects of the modern lifestyle have an answer in the "slow food" movement. This is an organization emphasizing the appreciation of food well prepared and enjoyed leisurely. Founded in Italy in 1986, they now have chapters around the world, appropriately called "convivia." Part of the idea is to consider not so much *what* to eat, or *how much* to eat, but rather how to eat *well*. It certainly isn't necessary to run out and join a formal organization though; a simpler solution might be to just make a point of offering a toast with each meal, which would serve as a sort of speed bump and a reinforcement of the communal aspect of dining. And if we recall the

---

*   Wine in Peace and War, 1947, Welbecson Press Ltd, London. A delightful and only semi-satirical book.

An Organic Matter

Is organic wine better for you? Certainly many consumers believe in the benefits of organic foods. Although still less than 3% of retail sales in the U.S., the organic food movement is forecast to grow rapidly, and an increasing number of wine growers are getting in on the act too. Although chemists define "organic chemistry" as anything involving the carbon-based molecules that lifeforms are made of (and students everywhere define it as just a really difficult class), the popular use of the term defines organic food as "produced without using most conventional pesticides; fertilizers made with synthetic ingredients or sewer sludge; bioengineering; or ionizing radiation". (A related but distinctly different method is known as "biodynamic" which also emphasizes avoidance of synthetic fertilizers and pesticides. This philosophy seems to apply most commonly to wine growing.)

There is good theoretical reason to support the idea that organically grown grapes might make wine with better health benefits. Since the polyphenols in the skins are produced in response to stressing the vines, grapes which need to fend for themselves to a greater degree without the aid of synthetic fertilizers or pesticides might make more of them. There isn't much direct evidence of this however, possibly because the studies just haven't been done. A few reports suggest that some fruits and berries grown organically do indeed have more polyphenols, but follow-up dietary tests found no improvement in antioxidant measures in the blood.

Getting the right polyphenol concentration in the wine is a balancing act regardless of growing methods; stress the vines too much and the results can be disastrous, not enough and the wine is thin and uninteresting, not to mention lacking in health benefits. I do know that some of my favorite wines are grown biodynamically, but whether I am healthier for it or not I can only speculate.

importance of cultural and community engagement in anti-aging, makes a lot of sense.

Still not convinced? Wine is at it's essence an agricultural product, and in fact one of the few things that we consume about which we know anything specific regarding its source and processing. Imagine instead of the popular wine country pilgrimages people flocked to specific orchards to see the quality of the soil, the slope of the terrain, and pruning techniques for Farmer John's pear or apple trees. At what stage of ripeness were they picked? This information is often right on the wine label, but good luck finding truly tree-ripened fruit in a grocery store, or any useful data on the growing conditions of the pineapples that went into the can of juice. We would probably be healthier if we paid as much attention to the other things we consume as we often do with wine.

Though the processed food-like products that we consume today bear little resemblance to traditional fare, habits of how and what we eat and drink have been steeped in cultural and even religious significance for as long as there have been cultures and religions. The rituals and customs of the table are central to how we live and our enjoyment of life, and parsing the question of wine into a different category threatens that relationship. So while it may be theoretically possible to compress complete nutrition into a pill, that doesn't make it a meal. A dinner needs to be more than a pit stop in the rat race. And the benefits of wine aren't reducible to mere chemistry either; even if you could put all your wine polyphenols into a pill, your wine "prescription" would need to be taken with meals for optimal effect.

Like my good friend the doctor, I have eaten little animal food . . . I double, however, the doctor's glass and a half of wine, even treble it with a friend.
                                   —Thomas Jefferson, in a letter at age 72

Digestif

A Toast to your Health

If for some reason wine's anti-aging promise fails to reach its full potential, perhaps one can take comfort in the possibility of wine in the afterlife. A document known as the Old Kingdom Pyramid Texts mentions that a "king's principle beverage after joining the gods in the western sky is wine." (Royal tombs were stocked with substantial wine cellars for the journey.) In China, where cultural traditions foster respect for one's forebears, we are told of the practice of presenting heated wine and other offerings to ancestral spirits, so that the aromas (aromatic polyphenols) would lure them down where they could commune with the living and restore harmony. The Koran promises devout Muslims "rivers of wine" in the next life, a reward perhaps for abstinence in this one. And good Christians can probably count on an eternity of fine wine, given the central position it occupies in their practices.

The angels do have their allocation, after all. In the Middle Ages, when the Roman Catholic church had stewardship of so much of the wine industry through monastery vineyard properties, aging in oak barrels was introduced. It is told that a pope or other high-ranking official became suspicious about gradual loss of wine from the barrels as the wine was aged. Assuming that it was being surreptitiously siphoned, he assigned a certain trusted monk to spend two years in the cellar, without leaving, to keep an eye on things and apprehend the wine thief. When asked to explain the continuing disappearance of wine under his watch, the reply was "It must be the angels' share." This evaporative loss is something that winemakers ever since have accepted as justifiable payment in exchange for divine complicity.

But it is wine's earthly properties that we celebrate here. We may ask in all fairness why the concept of "healthy drinking" is still held by so many to be an oxymoron. We lament the widening gulf between the disappearing culture of wine with dinner, and our expanding knowledge of its remarkable health benefits. How is it that people had healthier habits about wine hundreds, even thousands of years ago?

After a lecture I gave on this subject a couple of years ago to a group of doctors, one of them made a comment afterward that I thought was telling. He said something like: "Your points about wine and health were very compelling, but my wife and I don't drink at home because we don't want to set a bad example for our children." I wondered, if parents don't set an example of healthy drinking, wine as a part of a meal with family, what other models will our children emulate? Television commercials? Kegger parties at college?

Americans, I suppose, may have once had an excuse because of our history, but no longer. True, the will to re-create a wine-friendly life still tows the burden of our Prohibition legacy, and our relationship with wine was always tenuous anyway because of the difficulties our pilgrim forebears had in establishing viticulture here. Now, though, we have ignited a worldwide effort that has already blown wide open an exciting and promising new field of research. For thousands of years wine has held a secret sought by pharaohs, emperors, and kings, and the very real possibility that we can extend life by decades now seems within our grasp.

We can date the birth of the new era in wine research to the 1979 article in *The Lancet* by St. Leger, Cochrane, and Moore of Cardiff; their observation that heart disease inversely correlated with wine consumption set the foundation for what became known as the French Paradox more than a decade later. They had no idea at the time why this should be the case, but to conclude the article they noted: "If wine is ever found to contain a constituent protective against I.H.D. [ischemic heart disease] then we consider it almost a sacrilege that this constituent should be isolated. The medicine is already in a highly palatable form (as every connoisseur will confirm.)" In retrospect, the question of some special element in wine is simply too intriguing to ignore, at least for the scientist with an open and inquisitive mind. The question now is whether we will have the wisdom to wield this new knowledge well.

We can anticipate updates in the coming years on the studies currently in progress looking at resveratrol and the longevity effect. The fact that it works in mammals (mice) is encouraging for us humans, though we must note that the doses required appear to multiply greatly as the organism in question becomes more complex. Studies in primates and other animals with a longer natural lifespan will take decades to complete, and we are far from knowing what a safe and effective dose is, if there is indeed one. But we do know that red wine fights a host of degenerative conditions in dietary doses, and in a form that is not only palatable but enjoyable. We know that wine not only plays a part in a health-oriented lifestyle, but we can make the case for a starring role.

Wine is more than a drink, more than a food, more than a miracle life-extending pharmaceutical supplement. Even the business side of wine has a long tradition of involvement in promoting health. The oldest and reputedly the greatest charity sale in the world is the Hospices de Beaune in Burgundy, dating to 1859. The Hospice was originally founded in the mid-fifteenth century for the care of the old, the needy, and the sick, and supported by vineyard lands for centuries. A great many healthcare charity auctions around the world today are supported by the wine industry, with proceeds in the millions of dollars. Generosity, camaraderie, and passion for life are components of wine as much as any chemical compounds.

So a toast to your health is proffered with chapter and verse to back it up. We can cheer the thought that wine can help us live longer, and hope that its boost to our brain power will give us the good sense to do something meaningful with our bonus years.

> *When wine enlivens the heart, may friendship surround the table.*
>
> —Oliver Wendell Holmes

Addendum

As this edition is being prepared to go to press, there are 10 clinical trials underway for resveratrol. Six of these are for cancer, either prevention, therapy after surgery, or with chemotherapy, and two for Alzheimer's (prevention and treatment). A database for clinical trials can be found at www.clinicaltrials.gov, and running commentary on these and more developments in wine and health related matters at my blog www.healthandwine.blogspot.com.

Selected References

Chapter 1

1. Das DK, Ursini F. Preface. Ann N.Y. Acad Sci 2002;957:7. *Volume 957 of the Annals of the New York Academy of Sciences is titled "Alcohol and wine in health and disease". Selected articles are referenced here.*
2. Vintani PG. Fragments of tradition: revisiting the virtues of wine. Drugs Exptl Clin Res. 1999;XXV(2/3):163
3. Kladstrup D, Kladstrup P. Wine and War. Broadway Books 2001; New York
4. McGovern PE. Ancient Wine. Princeton University Press 2003; Princeton, NJ
5. Phillips R. A Short History of Wine. Harper Collins. 2000; New York. *A comprehensive history of wine.*
6. Norrie P. Corrupt captains and convicts. Ann N.Y. Acad Sci 2002 May;957:333. *An interesting slice of the Australian wine history as told by Australian physician Phillip Norie.*

Chapter 2

1. Harman D. A theory based on free radical and radiation chemistry. J Gerontol 1956;11:298. *The original theory of oxidation and aging.*
2. Ames BN, Shigenaga MK, Hagen TM. Oxidants, antioxidants, and the degenerative diseases of aging. Proc Natl Acad Sci USA 1993;90:7915

3. Olshansky SJ, Carnes BA. The quest for immortality: Science at the frontiers of aging. W.W. Norton & Co. 2001; New York

4. Scientific American. The truth about human aging. Position statement on human aging. 2002 May 13; www.scientificamerican.com. *A panel of 51 of the top researchers in aging express concern about the proliferation of pseudoscientific antiaging products.*

5. Allard M, Lebre V, Robine JM. Jeanne Calment: From Van Gogh's time to ours: 122 extraordinary years. W.H. Freeman & Co. 1998; New York

6. Olshansky SJ, Carnes BA, Cassel C. In search of Methuselah: Estimating the upper limits of human longevity. Science 1990;250:634

7. Butler RN, Fossel M et al. Anti-aging medicine: Efficacy and safety of hormones and antioxidants Geriatrics 2000;55:48

8. de Gray ADNJ. The foreseeability of real anti-aging medicine: focusing the debate. Exp Gerontol 2003 Sept;38(9):927

9. Burzynski SR. Aging: gene silencing or gene activation? Med Hypotheses 2005;64(1):201. *Discusses genetic switching and control with polyphenols.*

10. National Institute on Aging. Aging under the microscope. National Institutes of Health September 2002; publication No. 02-2756

11. Vivekananthan DP, Penn MS et al. Use of antioxidant vitamins for the prevention of cardiovascular disease: meta-analysis of randomised trials. Lancet 2003 Jun 14;361(9374):2017. *No benefit to use of antioxidant vitamins.*

12. Treatment of atherosclerosis in the new millennium: is there a role for vitamin E? Meagher EA. Prev Cardiol 2003 Spring;6(2):85

13. Bagchi D, Sen CK et al. Molecular mechanisms of cardioprotection by a novel grape seed proanthocyanidin extract. Mutat Res 2003 Feb-Mar;523-524:87. *"Free radicals and oxidative stress play a crucial role in the pathophysiology of a broad spectrum of cardiovascular diseases..."*

14. Hennekens CH, Buring JE et al. Lack of effect of long-term supplementation with beta carotene on the incidence of malignant neoplasms and cardiovascular disease. NEJM 1996 May 2;334(18):1145. *The large scale trial involving more than 22,000 male physicians over 13 years.*

Chapter 3

1. Pearson TA. AHA science advisory: alcohol and heart disease. Circulation 1996;94(11):3023. *Wherein the American Heart Association concludes that "If no contraindications of alcohol consumption are present, consumption of alcohol (one or two drinks per day) may be considered safe."*

2. Berger K, Ajani UA et al. Light-to-moderate alcohol consumption and the risk of stroke among U.S. male physicians. NEJM 1999;341(21):1557. *Large multicenter study involving more than twenty-two thousand physician subjects, found overall risk of ischemic stroke reduced by 21% in drinkers compared to non-drinkers overall, with greatest reduction in the moderate drinking subset.*

3. Cabot RC. The relation of alcohol to arteriosclerosis. JAMA 1904;774

4. Haut MJ, Cowan DH. The effect of ethanol on hemostatic properties of human blood platelets. Am J Med 1974;56:22. *Early reference for anti-clotting effect of alcohol.*

5. Ernst N, Fisher M et al. The association of plasma high-density lipoprotein cholesterol with dietary intake and alcohol consumption. The Lipid Research Clinics program prevalence study. Circulation 1980;64(suppl IV):41

6. Stason WB, Neff RK et al. Alcohol consumption and nonfatal myocardial infarction. Am J Epidemiol 1976;104:603

7. Thornton J, Symes C, Heaton K. Moderate alcohol intake reduces bile cholesterol saturation and raises HDL cholesterol. Lancet 1983;2:819

8. Hennekens CH, Rosner B, Cole DS. Daily alcohol consumption and fatal coronary heart disease. Am J Epidemiol 1978;107:196

9. Klatsky AL, Friedman GD, Siegelaub AB. Alcohol consumption before myocardial infarction. Results from the Kaiser-Permanente epidemiologic study of myocardial infarction. Ann Intern Med 1974;81:294

10. Rosenberg L, Slone D et al. Alcoholic beverages and myocardial infarction in young women. Am J Public Health 1981;71:82

11. Yano K, Reed DM, McGhee DL. Ten-year incidence of coronary heart disease in the Honolulu Heart Program. Am J Epidemiol 1984;119:653

12. Kozarevic D, Vojvodic N et al. Frequency of alcohol consumption and morbidity and mortality. The Yugoslavia cardiovascular disease study. Lancet 1980;1:613. *Cohort study of more than 11,000 subjects.*

13. Kittner SJ, Garcia-Palmieri MR et al. Alcohol and coronary heart disease in Puerto Rico. Am J Epidemiol 1983;117:538

14. Gordon T, Kannel WB. Drinking habits and cardiovascular disease: The Framingham Study. Am Heart J 1983;105:667

15. Naimi TS, Brewer RD et al. Binge drinking among US adults. JAMA 2003 Jan 1;289(1):70. *Binge drinking episodes increased by 17% in the U.S. from 1993 to 2001, especially in young adults ages 18-25.*

16. Stampfer MJ, Colditz GA et al. A prospective study of moderate alcohol consumption and the risk of coronary disease and stroke in women. NEJM 1988;319(5):267. *The J-shaped curve applies for women as demonstrated in this report from Harvard based on the Nurses' Health Study of more than eighty-seven thousand subjects.*

17. Seltzer CC. "Conflicts of Interest" and "Political Science". J Clin Epidemiol 1997;50(5):627. *Dr. Seltzer reflects on the difficulties in bringing to light the Framingham data about alcohol and coronary disease in 1972.*

18. Mukamal KJ, Jadhav PP et al. Alcohol and hemostatic factors: Analysis of the Framingham offspring cohort. Circulation 2001;104:1367. *Light-to-moderate alcohol consumption was associated with reduced levels of several blood clotting factors and lower blood viscosity.*

19. Klatsky AL. Alcohol and cardiovascular diseases: A historical overview. Ann N.Y. Acad Sci 2002;957:7

20. Gaziano JM, Hennekens JH et al. Type of alcoholic beverage and risk of myocardial infarction. Am J Cardiol 1999;83:52. *From Harvard, analysis showing benefit of alcohol from any source for protection against heart attack.*

21. Gaziano JM, Buring JE et al. Moderate alcohol intake, increased levels of high-density lipoprotein and its subfractions, and decreased risk of myocardial infarction. NEJM 1993;329(25):1829

22. di Guissepe R, de Lorgeril M, Salen P, Laporte F, et al. Alcohol consumption and n-3 polyunsaturated fatty acids in healthy men and women from 3 European populations. Am J Clin Nutr 2009 Jan;89(1):354-62

23. de Lorgeril M, Salen P, Martin JL, Boucher F, de Leiris J. Interactions of wine drinking with omega-3 fatty acids in patients with coronary heart disease; a fish-like effect of moderate drinking. Am Heart J 2008 Jan;155(1):175-81. *This and the previous citation find that alcohol increases levels of heart-health omega-3 fatty acids.*

24. Krenz M, Cohen MV, Downey JM. The protective and anti-protective effects of ethanol in a myocardial infarct model. Ann N.Y. Acad Sci 2002;957:103

25. Ford G. The science of healthy drinking. Wine Appreciation Guild 2003; South San Francisco, CA. *Comprehensive overview and annotated bibliography by the late Gene Ford.*

26. Mann K, Hermann D, Heinz A. One hundred years of alcoholism: The twentieth century. Alcohol Alcoholism 2000;35(1):10

27. Powers JR, Young AF. Longitudinal analysis of alcohol consumption and health of middle-aged women in Australia. Addiction 2008 mar;103(3):424. *Moderate drinkers who increase or decrease their alcohol consumption suffer a deterioration of their overall health status.*

Chapter 4

1. Parks DA, Booyse FM. Cardiovascular protection by alcohol and polyphenols. Ann N.Y. Acad Sci 2002;957:115

2. Sato M, Maulik N, Das DK. Cardioprotection with alcohol: Role of both alcohol and polyphenol antioxidants. Ann N.Y. Acad Sci 2002;957:174

3. De Gaetano G, De Curtis A et al. Antithrombotic effect of polyphenols in experimental models: A mechanism of reduced vascular risk by moderate wine consumption. Ann N.Y. Acad Sci 2002;957:146 *Meta-analysis and review.*

4. Nigdikar SV, Williams NR, et al. Consumption of red wine polyphenols reduces the susceptibility of low-density lipoproteins to oxidation in vivo. Am J Clin Nutr 1998;68:258

5. Renaud SC, Guegen R et al. Wine, Beer, and mortality in middle-aged men from eastern France. Arch Intern Med 1999;159:1865. *Upon which the "French paradox" was based.*

6. Renaud S, De Lorgeril M. Wine, alcohol, platelets, and the French paradox for coronary heart disease. Epidemiology 1992 Jun 20;339:1523. *Renaud's defense of the French paradox following the "60 minutes" report.*

7. Heberden W. Some account of a disorder of the breast. Med Trans R Coll Physicians (London) 1786;2:59. *The original description of angina pectoris, noting that wine provides a degree of symptomatic relief.*

8. St. Leger AS, Cochrane AL, Moore F. Factors associated with cardiac mortality in developed countries with particular reference to the consumption of wine. Lancet 1979 May 12;1017. *Countries with higher per capita wine consumption have lower rates of heart disease and vice-versa.*

9. Gronbaek M, Becker U et al. Type of alcohol consumed and mortality from all causes, coronary heart disease, and cancer. Ann Intern Med 2000 Sept 19;133(6):411. *The J-shaped curve shows a clear advantage for wine drinkers as compared to other types of alcohol consumed.*

10. Cordova AC, Jackson LM et al. The cardiovascular protective effect of red wine. J Am Coll Surg 2000;200(3):428. *Review article from Yale.*

11. De Lorimer AA. Alcohol, wine, and health. Am J Surg 2000;180:357

12. Källberg H, Jacobsen S, Bengtsson C et al. Alcohol consumption is associated with decreased risk of rheumatoid arthritis: Results from two Scandinavian case-control studies. Ann Rheum Dis 2008 Jun 5

13. Mukamal KJ. Alcohol consumption in older adults and Medicare costs. Health Care Financing Review 2006 Spring

Chapter 5

1. Mokni M, Limam F et al. Strong cardioprotective effect of resveratrol, a red wine polyphenol, on isolated rat hearts after ischemia/reperfusion injury. Arch Biochem Biophys 2007 Jan 1;457(1):1. *From Tunisia.*

2. Kiziltepe U, Turan NN et al. Resveratrol, a red wine polyphenol, protects spinal cord from ischemia-reperfusion injury. J Vasc Surg 2004 Jul;40(1):138. *From Ankara, Turkey, a study in rats finding dramatic improvement in post-ischemia spinal cord function.*

3. Corder R, Douthwaite JA et al. Endothelin-1 synthesis reduced by red wine. Nature 2001 Dec 20-27;414(6866):863

4. Rahman I, Biswas SK, Kirkham PA. Regulation of inflammation and redox signaling by dietary polyphenols. Biochem Pharmacol 2006 Aug 17; *Overview article of polyphenol antioxidant properties from India and the U.K.*

5. Gambuti A, Strollo D et al. trans-Resveratrol, quercetin, (+)-catechin, and (−)-epicatechin content in south Italian monovarietal wines: relationship with maceration time and marc pressing during winemaking. J Agric Food Chem 2004 Sept 8;52(18):5747. *Resveratrol content increases steadily throughout the maceration period up to 12 days.*

6. Takkouche B, Reguiera-Mendez C et al. Intake of wine, beer, and spirits and the risk of clinical common cold. Am J Epidemiol 2002 may 1;155(9):853

7. Audera C, Patulny RV et al. Mega-dose vitamin C in treatment of common cold: a randomised controlled trial. Med J Aust 2001 Oct 1;175970;359. *No differences in duration or severity of colds with vitamin C.*

8. Noroozi M, Angerson WJ, Lean MEJ. Effects of flavonoids and vitamin C on oxidative DNA damage to human lymphocytes. Am J Clin Nutr 1998;67:1210. *Wine polyphenols esp. quercetin much more effective than vitamin C.*

9. Conti C, Mastromarino P et al. Anti-picornovirus activity of synthetic flavon-3-yl esters. Antivir Chem Chemother 1998 Nov;9(6):511

10. Blardi P, de Lalla A et al. Stimulation of endogenous adenosine release by oral administration of quercetin and resveratrol in man. Drugs Exptl Clin Res 1999;XXV(2/3):105

11. Sen CK, Khanna S et al. Oxygen, oxidants, and antioxidants in wound healing. An emerging paradigm. Ann N.Y. Acad Sci. 2002;957:239. *Wine polyphenols facilitate wound healing in this study from Ohio State University Medical Center.*

12. Lim I, Phan TT et al. Quercetin inhibits keloid and hypertrophic scar fibroblast proliferation and collagen production. ANZ J Surg 2003;73(Suppl.):A286

Chapter 6

1. Calabrese G. Nonalcoholic compounds of wine: The phytoestrogen resveratrol and moderate red wine consumption during menopause. Drugs Exptl Clin Res 1999;XXV9(2/3):111

2. Rucinski M, Ziolkowska A et al. Estradiol and resveratrol stimulating effect on oteocalcin, but not osteonectin and collagen-1 alpha gene expression in primary culture of rat calvarial osteoblast-like cells. Int J Mol Med 2006 Oct;18(4):565. *Study from the Poznan Medical University in Poland showing similarities between resveratrol and the estrogen estradiol in stimulating bone production cells.*

3. Gehm BD, McAndrews JM, Chien PY, Jameson JL. Resveratrol, a polyphenolic compound found in grapes and wine, is an agonist for the estrogen receptor. Proc Nat Acad Sci USA 1997;94:14138-43. *"Agonist" is the opposite of "antagonist" meaning that resveratrol stimulates estrogen receptors.*

4. Howitz KT, Bitterman KJ et al. Small molecule activators of sirtuins extend *Saccharomyces cerevisiae* lifespan. Nature 2003 Sept;425:191. *The report that identified resveratrol as a sirtuins activator.*

5. Baur JA, Pearson KJ et al. Resveratrol improves health and survival of mice on a high-calorie diet. Nature 2006 Nov 16:144(7117):337. *The most widely circulated news of the day.*

6. Su Jen-Liang, Yang Ching-Yao et al. Forkhead proteins is critical for BMP-2 regulation and anti-tumor activity of resveratrol. J Biol Chem 2007 Jul 6;282(27): 19385. *From China Medical University*

in Taiwan and Vanderbilt in Nashville, this paper explains how resveratrol protects against osteoporosis and cancer.

7. Wood JG, Rogina B et al. Sirtuin activators mimic caloric restriction and delay ageing in metazoans. Nature 2004 August;430:686

8. de la Lastra CA, Villegas I. Reveratrol as an anti-inflammatory and anti-aging agent: Mechanisms and clinical implications. Molecular Nutrition Food Res 2005;49(5):405. *Review article from the University of Seville, Spain.*

9. Valenziano DR, Terzibasi E et al. Resveratrol prolongs lifespan and retards the onset of age-related markers in a short-lived vertebrate. Curr Biol 2006 Feb 7;16(3):296. *From Italy, a study demonstrating the resveratrol longevity effect on fish.*

10. Baur JA, Sinclair DA. Therapeutic potential of resveratrol: the in vivo evidence. Nat Rev Drug Discov 2006 Jun;5(6):493. *Comprehensive review from Harvard.*

11. Oderdoerffer P, Michan S, McVay M et al. SIRT1 redistribution on chromatin promotes genomic stability but alters gene expression during aging. 2008 Nov;135(5):907-918. *Update from Sinclair's group describing in greater detail the role of sirtuins in countering the aging process by stabilizing the proteins that control DNA gene expression.*

12. Tutel'yan VA, Gapparov MM et al. Flavonoids and resveratrol as regulators of Ah-receptor activity: protection from dioxin toxicity. Bull Exp Bio Med 2003 Dec;136(6):533. *From the Russian Academy of Medical Sciences in Moscow, finding possible use of wine polyphenols to treat cases of dioxin poisoning.*

13. Palamara AT, Nencioni L et al. Inhibition of Influenza A virus replication by resveratrol. J Infect Dis 2005;191:1719. *From Rome, finding strong anti-viral effect of resveratrol.*

14. Borra MT, Smith BC, Denu JM. Mechanism of human SIRT1 activation by resveratrol. J Biol Chem 2005 Apr 29;280(17):17187. *Investigation of the molecular pathways for activation of the sirtuins enzyme system responsible for the longevity effect.*

15. Ingram DK, Zhu M et al. Calorie restriction mimetics: an emerging research field. Aging Cell 2006 Apr;5(2):97. *From the Laboratory of Experimental Gerontology at the National Institute on Aging.*

16. Chan MM. Antimicrobial effect of resveratrol on dermatophytes and bacterial pathogens of the skin. Biochem Pharmacol 2002 Jan 15;63(2):99-104

17. Baxter RA. Anti-aging properties of resveratrol: review and report of a potent new antioxidant skin care formulation. J Cosmetic Dermatol 2008;7:2-7

18. Baliga MS, Katiyar SK. Chemoprevention of photocarcinogenesis by selected dietary botanicals. Photochem Photobiol Sci 2006 Feb;5(2):243-53. *Resveratrol prevents skin cancer from ultraviolet light exposure.*

19. Ma ZH, Ma QY. Resveratrol: a medical drug for acute pancreatitis. World J Gastroenterol 2005 June 7;11(21):3171. *From China.*

20. Bertelli AAE, Migliori M et al. Resveratrol, a component of wine and grapes, in the prevention of kidney disease. Ann N.Y. Acad Sci 2002;957:230. *From Milan, Pisa, and the University of Connecticut.*

21. Bertelli A, Falchi M, Dib B, Pini E, Mukherjee S, Das DK. Analgesic resveratrol? Antioxid Redox Signal 2008 Mar;10(3):403-4. *The authors speculate that resveratrol may work as an analgesic by inhibiting COX enzymes.*

22. Lei M, Liu SQ, Liu YL. Resveratrol protects bone marrow mesenchymal stem cell derived chondrocytes cultured on chitosan-gelatin scaffolds from the inhibitory effect of interleukin-1 beta. Acta Pharmacol Sin 2008 Nov;29(11):1350-6. *In this experimental model of arthritis, researchers from the University of Wuhan in China, resveratrol protected cartilage cells from destruction.*

23. Csaki C, Keshishzadeh N, Fischer K, Shakibachi M. Regulation of inflammation signaling by resveratrol in human chondrocytes in vitro. Biochem Pharmacol 2008 Feb 1;75(3):677-87. *From Munich, Germany.*

24. Elmali N, Bavsol O, Harma A, Esenkava I, Mizrak B. Effects of resveratrol in inflammatory arthritis. Inflammation 2007 Apr;30(1-2):1-6. *From Turkey, evidence of resveratrol's ability to mitigate inflammatory destruction of cartilage when injected directly into the joint in a rabbit arthritis model.*

25. Li X, Phillips FM, An HS, et al. The action of resveratrol, a phytoalexin found in grapes, on the intervertebral disc. Spine 2008 Nov 15;33(24):2586-95. *Anyone with a history of back pain from disc problems will be encouraged by this study which found that resveratrol aids repair and regeneration of damaged discs in an experimental model.*

Chapter 7

1. Sumpio BE, Cordova AC et al. Green tea, the "Asian paradox," and cardiovascular disease. J Am Coll Surg 2006 May;202(5):813. *Review article on tea polyphenols and cardiovascular disease.*
2. Achike FI, Kwan CY. Nitric Oxide, human diseases and the herbal products that affect the nitric oxide signaling pathway. Clin Exp Pharmacol Physiol 2003 Sept;30(9):605. *Summary of the roles of NO and polyphenols.*
3. Aviram M, Dornfeld L. Pomegranate juice consumption inhibits serum angiotensin converting enzyme activity and reduces systolic blood pressure. Atherosclerosis 2001 Sep;158(1):195-8
4. Aviram M, Rosenblat M, Gaitini D et al. Pomegranate juice consumption for 3 years by patients with carotid artery stenosis reduced common carotid intima-media thickness, blood pressure and LDL oxidation. Clin Nutr 2004 Jun;23(3):423-33. *Atherosclerotic plaques were reduced in subjects drinking pomegranate juice.*
5. Phytochemical and nutrient composition of the freeze-dried Amazonian palm berry, Euterpe oleraceae mart. (acai). Schauss AG, Wu X et al. J Agric Food Chem 2006 Nov 1;54(22):8598. *Most of the polyphenols in acai juice are anthocyanins and proanthocyanidins.*
6. Anderson LF, Jacobs DR et al. Consumption of coffee is associated with reduced risk of death attributed to inflammatory and cardiovascular diseases in the Iowa Women's Health Study. Am J Clin Nutr 2006 May;83(5):1039. *This is the University of Oslo analysis that found women who drank 1-3 cups of coffee daily were 25% less likely to die of cardiovascular disease, improving to 33% lower mortality of inflammatory diseases at 4-5 cups.*

7. Lee WJ, Zhu BT. Inhibition of DNA methylation by caffeic acid and chlorogenic acid, two common catechol-containing coffee polyphenols. Carcinogenesis 2006 Feb;27(2):269

8. Fujioka K, Shibamoto T. Quantitation of volatiles and nonvolatile acids in an extract from coffee beverages: correlation with antioxidant activity. J Agric Food Chem 2006 Aug 9;54(16):6054

9. Pereira MA, Parker ED, Folsom AR. Coffee consumption and risk of type 2 diabetes mellitus: an 11-year prospective study of 28 812 postmenopausal women. Arch Intern Med 2006 Jun 26;166(12):1311. *From the Iowa Women's Health Study, 6 or more cups meant 22% lower risk of diabetes.*

10. Pellegrini MN, Serafini M et al. Total antioxidant capacity of plant foods, beverages and oils consumed in Italy by three different in vitro assays. J Nutr 2003 Sept;113:2812. *From the University of Parma, a reference for dietary polyphenol antioxidants.*

Chapter 8

1. Grønbaeck M, Becker U et al. Type of alcohol consumed and mortality from all causes, coronary heart disease, and cancer. Ann Internal Med 2000;133(6):411

2. Renaud S, Guégen R et al. Wine, beer, and mortality in middle-aged men from eastern France. Arch Intern Med 1999;159:1865

3. Soleas GJ, Grass L et al. A comparison of the anticarcinogenic properties of four red wine polyphenols. Clin Biochem 2006 May;39(5):492. *This report from the Quality Assurance Department of the Liquor Control Board of Ontario, Canada (!) concludes that resveratrol holds the most potential as a chemopreventive agent.*

4. Schoonen WM, Salinas CA et al. Alcohol consumption and risk of cancer in middle-aged men. Epidemiology 2005 Jan 1;113(1):133. *Widely reported study from the Fred Hutchinson Cancer Research Center in Seattle, finding a dose-response correlation between red wine consumption and lower risk of prostate cancer, no correlations with other alcoholic drinks.*

5. Longnecker MP. Alcoholic beverage consumption in relation to risk of breast cancer: Meta-analysis and review. Cancer Causes and

Control 1994;5:73 *This landmark paper finds a correlation between breast cancer and alcohol intake, but inferences for low levels of wine consumption not conclusive.*

6. Zhang Y, Kreger BE et al. Alcohol consumption and risk of breast cancer: the Framingham Study revisited. Am J Epidemiol 1999;149(2):93

7. Nagata C, Mizoue T, Tanaka K et al. Alcohol drinking and breast cancer risk: An evaluation based on a systematic review of epidemiologic evidence among the Japanese population. Jpn J Clin Oncol 2007 Aug;37(8):568-74. *Finding "...epidemiologic evidence on the association between alcohol drinking and breast cancer risk remains insufficient ..."*

8. Bessaoud F, Daures JP. Patterns of alcohol (especially wine) consumption and breast cancer risk: a case-control study among a population in Southern France. Ann Epidemiol. 2008 Jun;18(6):467-75. *Case-control study finding lower risk of breast cancer in moderate wine drinkers.*

9. Rohan TE, Jain MG et al. Dietary folate consumption and breast cancer risk. J National Cancer Inst 2000;92(3):266

10. Boffetta P, Garfinkel L. Alcohol drinking and mortality among men enrolled in an American Cancer Society prospective study. Epidemiology 2000;1(5):342

11. Kampa M, Hatzoglu A et al. Wine antioxidant polyphenols inhibit the proliferation of human prostate cancer cell lines. Nutrition and Cancer 2000;37(2):223

12. Damianaki A, Bakogeorgou E et al. Potent inhibitory action of red wine polyphenols on human breast cancer cells. J Cellular Biochem 2000;78:429. *This is the report that really started it all, from Castanas and colleagues from the University of Crete in Greece.*

13. Fuchs CS, Stampfer MJ et al. Alcohol consumption and mortality among women. NEJM 1995;332:1245. *A collaborative prospective study from Harvard and other Boston area institutions, concluding light-to-moderate drinking was associated with a lower mortality rate for women, primarily due to cardiovascular benefits, while heavy drinking correlated to higher mortality from breast cancer and cirrhosis of the liver.*

14. Dorai T, Aggarwal BB. Role of chemopreventive agents in cancer therapy. Cancer letters 2004;215(2):129. *An excellent review of the various chemopreventive mechanisms of phenolics, from the New York Medical College and the M.D. Anderson Cancer Center at the University of Texas.*

15. Inoue M, Tajima K et al. Tea and coffee consumption and the risk of digestive tract cancers: data from a comparative case-referent study in Japan. Cancer Causes Control 1998 Mar;9(2):209. *A large case-control study finding that higher levels of tea consumption (more than 7 cups per day) was associated with lowered risk of stomach cancer, and 3 or more cups of coffee per day was linked to lower rates of colon cancer.*

16. Wu AH, Yu MC et al. Green tea and risk of breast cancer in Asian Americans. Int J Cancer 2003 Sept 10;106(4):574. *Drinkers of green tea, but not black tea, had lower rates of breast cancer in this analysis from the University of Southern California Keck School of Medicine.*

17. Rezk YA, Balulad SS et al. Use of resveratrol to improve the effectiveness of cisplatin and doxorubicin: study in human gynecologic cancer cell lines and in rodent heart. Am J Obstet Gynecol 2006 May;194(5)e23-6. *Study from the Albany Medical College showing enhanced effectiveness of chemotherapeutic agents on cancer cells in culture, and less toxicity on mouse heart tissue cells (cardiac toxicity a troublesome side effect of these drugs).*

18. Fulda S, Debatin KM. Resveratrol modulation of signal transduction in apoptosis and cell survival: A mini-review. Cancer Detect Prev 2006;30(3):217. *A concise discussion of the multiple signaling pathways with cancer cells affected by resveratrol.*

19. Wolter F, Ulrich S, Stein J. Molecular mechanisms of the chemopreventive effects of resveratrol and its analogs in colorectal cancer: key role of polyamines. J Nutr 2004;134:3219. *From the J.W. Goethe University in Frankfur,t Germany, an overview of chemopreventive actions of wine phenolics via signal transduction pathways.*

20. Niles RM, McFarland M et al. Resveratrol is a potent inducer of apoptosis in human melanoma cells. Cancer Lett 2003 Feb 20;190(2):157

21. Ellison RC. Balancing the risks and benefits of moderate drinking. Ann N.Y. Acad Sci 2002;957:1

22. Palmieri L, Mameli M, Ronca G. Effect of resveratrol and some other natural compounds on tyrosine kinase activity and on cytolysis. Drugs Exptl Clin Res 1999;XXV(2/3):79

23. Bhat KPL, Pezzuto JM. Cancer chemopreventive activity of resveratrol. Ann N.Y. Acad Sci 2002;957:210

24. Fugita H, Koshida K et al. Cyclooxygenase-2 promotes prostate cancer progression. Prostate 2002 Nov 1;53(3):232

25. Singh-Ranger G, Mokbel K. Currrent concepts in cyclo-oxygenase inhibition in breast cancer. J Clin Pharm Ther 2002 Oct;27(5):321

26. Sweeney CJ, Marshall MS et al. Cyclo-oxygenase-2 expression in primary cancers of the lung and bladder compared to normal adjacent tissue. Cancer Detect Prev 2002;26(3):238

27. Kohno H, Nagasue N, Rahman MA. COX-2—a target for preventing hepatic carcinoma? Expert Opin Ther Targets 2002 Aug;6(4):483

28. Lin DT, Subbaramaiah K et al. Cyclooxygenase-2: a novel molecular target for the prevention and treatment of head and neck cancer. Head Neck 2002 Aug;24(8):792

29. Howe LR, Dannenberg AJ. A role for cyclo-oxygenase inhibitors in the prevention and treatment of cancer. Semin Oncol 2002 Jun; 29(3 Suppl 11):111

30. Garg AK, Buchholtx TA, Aggarwal BB. Chemosensitization and radiosensitization of tumors by plant polyphenols. Antioxid Reox Signal 2005; Nov-Dec7(11-12):1630. *A review article from the M.D. Anderson Cancer Center at the University of Texas, discussing how polyphenols increase cancer susceptibility to chemotherapy and radiation therapy while minimizing toxicity.*

31. Simopoulos AP. The traditional diet of Greece and cancer. Eur J Cancer Prev 2004 Jun;13(3):219

32. Lambert JD, Hong J et al. Inhibition of carcinogenesis by polyphenols: evidence from laboratory investigations. Am J Clin Nutr 2005; 81(1):284S. *Report from the First International Conference on Polyphenols and Health, in Vichy, France, November 2004.*

33. Schlachterman A, Valle F, Wall KM, Azios NG, Castillo L, Morell L, Washington AV, Cubano LA, Dharmawardhane SF. Combined

resveratrol, quercetin, and catechin treatment reduces breast tumor growth in a nude mouse model. Transl Oncol. 2008 Mar;1(1):19-27. *See below.*

34. Castillo-Pichardo L, Martínez-Montemayor MM, Martínez JE, Wall KM, Cubano LA, Dharmawardhane S. Inhibition of mammary tumor growth and metastases to bone and liver by dietary grape polyphenols. Clin Exp Metastasis. 2009 Mar 18. [Epub ahead of print]. *This research from the School of Medicine, University of Puerto Rico, San Juan, showed that wine polyphenols together, in doses corresponding to healthy wine consumption, were more effective against cancer cells than any one alone – including resveratrol.*

Chapter 9

1. Truelson T, Thudium D, Grønbaek M. Amount and type of alcohol and risk of dementia. Neurology 2002;59:1319. *Report from the Copenhagen City Heart Study; concluded that beer and spirits drinkers were at increased risk, wine drinkers at lower risk compared to nondrinkers.*

2. Lindsay J, Laurin D et al. Risk factors for Alzheimer's disease: a prospective analysis from the Canadian study of health and aging. A. J Epidemiol 2002 Sept 1;156(5):445. *A prospective analysis of risk factors for Alzheimer's disease, finding that red wine, NSAID's, coffee, and exercise were associated with lower risk.*

3. Zuccala G, Onder G et al. Dose-related impact of alcohol consumption on cognitive function in advanced age: results of a multicenter survey. Alcohol Clin Exp Res 2001 Dec;25(12):1743. *This study from the Catholic University of Rome found that men drinking up to one liter of wine and women drinking up to a half-liter daily had better cognitive performance.*

4. Commenges D, Scotet V et al. Intake of flavonoids and risk of dementia. Eur J Epidemiol 2000 Apr;16(4):357. *Serge Renaud's study from the Institut National de la Santéet de la Recherche Médicale in Bordeaux.*

5. McDowell I. Alzheimer's disease: insights from epidemiology. Aging (Milano) 2001 Jun;13(3):143. *Overview of predisposing and protective factors for Alzheimer's, from the University of Ottawa, Canada; risk*

factors include lower education level and a specific genetic marker (apoliporoteinE-epsilon4 allele); protective agents are exercise, NSAID's, B vitamins (esp. folate) and red wine.

6. Elias PK, Elias MF et al. Alcohol consumption and cognitive performance in the Framingham Heart Study. Am J Epidemiol 1999;150(6):580

7. Boothby LA, Doering PL. Vitamin C and vitamin E for Alzheimer's disease. Ann Pharmacother 2005 Dec;39(12):2073. *A comprehensive review article from the Harrison School of Pharmacy at Auburn University; concludes that vitamins C and E are ineffective at reducing lower risk, though potentially a small effect in combination; meta-analysis concludes that doses of vitamin E in excess of 400 units daily associated with increased mortality risk.*

8. Schroeter H, Williams RJ et al. Phenolic antioxidants attenuate neuronal cell death following uptake of oxidized low-density lipoprotein. Free Rad Bio Med 2000 Dec 15;29(12):1222

9. Kumar A, Naidu PS, Seghal N, Padi SS. Neuroprotective effects of resveratrol against intracerebroventricular colchicines-induced cognitive impairment and oxidative stress in rats. Pharmacology 2007;79(1):17-26. *One way to really mess up a rat is by injecting colchicine into the brain, which causes extensive oxidative damage and kills nerve cells. Add resveratrol to their diet and it isn't nearly so bad though.*

10. Ono K, Yoshiike Y et al. Potent anti-amyloidogenic and fibril-destabilizing effects of polyphenols *in vitro*: implications for the prevention and therapeutics of Alzheimer's disease. J Neurochem 2003;87:172. *Study from Japan finding that wine polyphenols myricetin, morin, quercetin, kaempferol, catechin, and epicatechin all had anti-amyloid effects.*

11. Marambaudl P, Zhao H, Davies P. Resveratrol promotes clearance of Alzheimer's disease amyloid-ß peptides. J Biol Chem 2005 Nov 11; 280(45):37377

12. Anekonda TS. Resveratrol–A boon for treating Alzheimer's disease? Brain Research Reviews 2006 Sept;52(2):316. *Thoroughly referenced review article outlining multiple mechanisms by which resveratrol works against Alzheimer's.*

13. Savaskan E, Olivieri G et al. Red wine ingredient resveratrol protects from ß-amyloid toxicity. Gerontology 2003;49:380. *This report from the University of Basel, Switzerland, provided evidence from in vitro studies of the ability of resveratrol to protect brain cells from beta-amyloid-mediated oxidative damage.*

14. Wang Q, Xu J et al. Resveratrol protects against global cerebral ischemic injury in gerbils. Brain Res 2002 Dec 27;958(2):439. *These researchers demonstrated that resveratrol is able to penetrate the blood-brain barrier, and protect brain cells from the effects oxygen deprivation during a stroke.*

15. Tredici G, Miloso M et al. Resveratrol, MAP kinases, and neuronal cells: Might wine be a neuroprotectant? Drugs Exptl Clin Res 1999;XXV(2/3):99.

16. Ramassamy C. Emerging role of polyphenolic compounds in the treatment of neurodegenerative diseases: a review of their intracellular targets. Eur J Pharmacol 2006 Sept 1;545(5):51-64. *Detailed review of how polyphenols work inside cells to mitigate the cause of Alzheimer's and Parkinson's diseases.*

17. Miloso M, Bertelli AAE et al. Resveratrol-induced activation of the mitogen-activated protein kinases, ERK1 and ERK2, in human neuroblastoma SH-SY5Y cells. Neuroscience Letters 1999;264:141.

18. Zhang Q, Powers ET et al. Metabolite-initiated protein misfolding may trigger Alzheimer's disease. Proc Natl Acad Sci USA 2004 Apr 6;101(14):4752

19. Rossi L, Mazzitelli S, Arciello M, Capo CR, Rotilio G. Benefits from dietary polyphenols for brain aging and Alzheimer's disease. Neurochem Res 2008 Dec;33(12):2390–2400. *Review updating the state of knowledge regarding dietary resveratrol, catechins, and curcumin.*

20. Kim D, Nguyen MD, Dobbin MM et al. SIRT1 deacetylase protects against neurodegeneration in models for Alzheimer's disease and amyotrophic lateral sclerosis. EMBO J 2007 Jul 11;26(13):3169-79. *Resveratrol may have a role in preventing Alzheimer's and Lou Gehrig's disease by activating sirtuin, which promotes neuron survival in a mouse model.*

21. Wang J, Ho L, Zhao Z et al. Moderate consumption of Cabernet Sauvignon attenuates Abeta neuropathology in a mouse model of

Alzheimer's disease. FASEB J 2006 Nov;20(13):2313-2320. *If you have to be a mouse prone to Alzheimer's, this is the study you want to be in. Drinking cabernet significantly reduced deterioration of spatial memory function compared to alcohol alone or water. From Mount Sinai School of Medicine in New York.*

22. Baur JA, Sinclair DA. Therapeutic potential of resveratrol: the *in vivo* evidence. Nature Rev Drug Discov 2006 Jun;5(6):493

23. Mørtensen LH, Sørensen TI, Grønbaek M. Intelligence in relation to later beverage preference and alcohol intake. Addiction 2005 Oct;100(10):1445-52. *Smart people tend to prefer wine.*

24. Ingram DK, Young J, Mattison JA. Calorie restriction in nonhuman primates: assessing effects on brain and behavioral aging. Neuroscience 2005 Apr 14;145(4):1359-64

25. Zhuang H, Kim YS et al. Potential mechanism by which resveratrol, a red wine constituent, protects neurons. Ann N Y Acad Sci 2003 May;993:276. *Resveratrol protects brain cells by activating the enzyme that clears heme, an oxidant that mediates oxidative damage during stroke.*

26. Vingtdeux V, Dreses-Werringloer U, Zhao H, Davies P, Marambaud P. Therapeutic potential *of resveratrol in Alzheimer's disease. BMC Neurosci. 2008 Dec 3;9 Suppl 2:S6. A good review article.*

Chapter 10

1. Sies h, Stahl W, Sevanian A. Nutritional, dietary, and postprandial oxidative stress. J Nutr 2005 May;135(5):969

2. Laudan R. Birth of the modern diet. Scientific American Reports 2006 December;16(4):4

3. Ursini F, Sevanian A. Wine polyphenols and optimal nutrition. Ann N.Y. Acad Sci 2002;957:200. *Describes the Mediterranean diet connection between wine consumption with meals and reduction of postprandial oxidative damage.*

4. Johansen D, Friis K, Skovenborg E, Grønbaek M. Food buying habits of people who buy wine or beer: cross sectional study. BMJ 2006;332:519-22. *Wine buyers also buy healthier food items than beer purchasers.*

5. Dani C, Oliboni LS, Vanderlinde R, Bonatto D, Salvador M, Henriques JA. Phenolic content and antioxidant activities of white and purple juices manufactured with organically- or conventionally-produced grapes. Food Chem Toxicol 2007 Dec;45(12):2574-80. *From Brazil, this report suggests that organically-grown grapes have more polyphenols.*

6. Ikehara S, Iso H, Yamagishi K et al. Alcohol consumption, social support, and risk of stroke and coronary heart disease among Japanese men: The JPHC study. *Large cohort study showing that "Social support may enhance the beneficial effect of light-to-moderate alcohol consumption on risk of cardiovascular disease." So don't drink alone if you have a choice.*

Glossary

Alzheimer's disease – a degenerative disease of the brain typically affecting people over age 65; characterized by cognitive deterioration, behavioral changes, and progressive memory loss.

Antioxidant – a molecule capable of counteracting oxidation, a chemical reaction involving the transfer of electrons between molecules and often resulting in the formation of unstable molecules called *free radicals*, which may cause damage to DNA and other biomolecules. Oxidation is believed to be associated with many degenerative health conditions and accelerated aging, but trials of antioxidant vitamins have generally found no benefit.

Apoptosis – programmed cell death; apoptosis normally occurs, for example, as skin cells migrate from deeper in where they are formed to the surface, where they die and form a protective layer, which continuously exfoliates as new cells move up. Cancer cells bypass the apoptosis signals and grow out of control.

Beta-amyloid – an abnormal protein which accumulates in plaques and tangles in the brains of Alzheimer's victims.

Bioavailability – the degree to which a drug or nutrient is absorbed and delivered to the target tissue. Many discoveries which have promising capabilities in laboratory tests turn out to be ineffective as dietary supplements or drugs because they are broken down and excreted before they reach the organs where they might work.

Caloric restriction – a means of artificially extending lifespan by severely reducing the intake of calories. It has been demonstrated in animals with relatively short natural lifespans, but not yet proven in humans and other ape species. It is believed to occur by activation of enzymes called *sirtuins* which regulate energy metabolism.

Chemoprevention – lowering cancer risk by using compounds known to counteract carcinogenesis. Wine polyphenols work as chemoprevention agents by, for example, lowering the rate of DNA mutation from oxidation, or counteracting the effects of ultraviolet light on the skin.

COX enzymes – COX is short for *cyclo-oxygenase*, which exists in two forms, COX-1 and COX-2 (there os also a third form, called either COX-3 or COX 1b as it is a variant of COX-1). COX-1 converts precursors known as *eicosanoids* into prostaglandins and inflammatory molecules such as *thromboxane*. COX-2 has a high degree of association with cancer and inflammatory conditions. NSAID's such as ibuprofen inhibit both forms of COX, while COX-2 inhibitors such as Vioxx provide anti-inflammatory action but without the risk of stomach ulcers or bleeding disorders. Wine polyphenols are nonspecific COX inhibitors.

DES – Diethylstilbestrol, a synthetic estrogen hormone. It has a structure similar to resveratrol.

Error theory – a theory of aging based upon accumulation of DNA mutations, or errors, primarily from oxidative damage.

Estrogen – a class of female hormones with multiple effects; in terms of anti-aging, these include maintenance of bone mass, moisture retention in skin, and improved cholesterol profiles.

Flavonoid – a class of specific plant-derived polyphenols with impressive antioxidant capabilities and other properties.

Free radical – a molecule with an unpaired electron, which makes it highly reactive. In biological systems, most free radicals are derived from oxidative processes.

French paradox – a term first used on a CBS-TV "60 Minutes" report in which the French were noted to have low rates of heart disease despite unhealthy lifestyles, presumably because of their prodigious consumption of wine. This report jump-started the field of wine & health research.

In vitro – Literally, Latin for "in glass" meaning a test tube or more generally, in a laboratory as opposed to in a living organism. *In vitro* studies can yield extremely useful information but it doesn't always translate into the predicted effect in humans or other creatures.

In vivo – In living organisms, as in feeding resveratrol to obese rats to see if they get healthier.

Ischemia – lack of oxygen to tissue typically from inadequate delivery of oxygenated blood. Heart attacks and strokes are classic ischemic events.

Mediterranean diet – a lifestyle discovered during studies of health and longevity, found to be associated with low rates of degenerative diseases. The key elements are regular exercise, wine consumption with meals, olive oil, whole grains, and vegetables.

Meta-analysis – a means of determining whether a large number of research studies point to a definitive answer, by essentially combining the results of the studies into a sort of mega-study. Aberrant results tend to cancel out, while small but consistent findings emerge more clearly.

Phytoestrogen – a plant-derived molecule with estrogen-like properties. Resveratrol is a phytoestrogen.

Polyphenol – a biologic molecule with more than one phenol ring, a type of carbon hexagon. Polyphenols are often concentrated in the skins of berries and pigmented fruits. Many polyphenols are potent antioxidants.

Programmed theory – the companion to the *error theory*, the programmed theory of aging emphasizes the role of genetically programmed changes over an organism's life.

Quercetin – a flavonoid polyphenol, one of the better-studied molecules in the class.

Resveratrol – A stilbene polyphenol with a number of unique properties.

Senescence – progressive deterioration associated with aging.

Sirtuin – one of a series of enzymes (histone deacetylases) involved in regulation of energy metabolism and possibly associated with the caloric restriction-longevity effect.

Super-centenarian – someone 110 years or older

Xenohormosis – actions of hormone-like compounds not produced by the body, for example estrogen-like effects of resveratrol.

Index

continued on next page…